THE
ROYAL
EAGLE
MOM JOURNAL

A Faith-Filled Life Planner
and Prayer Journal for Christian Moms
Who Lead with Love

MAXINE EBANKS

THIS JOURNAL PLANNER BELONGS TO:

_____

EAGLE MOM

_____

DATE

_____

CONTACT

PSALM 103:5

The Lord satisfies you with good things; so that your youth is renewed like the eagles.

CONTENTS

PURPOSE

This journal planner is designed to inspire and encourage mothers to embrace their faith, nurture their well-being, and stay grounded in their roles as strong, loving caregivers. Through guided reflections, prayers, and self-care practices, you will cultivate a life of balance, purpose, and joy.

- Strengthen your spiritual connection and maintain a lifestyle of prayer.

- Stay positive and resilient in your mental, physical, and emotional well-being.

- Embrace your role as a Proverbs 31 and Titus 2 woman with grace, wisdom, and strength.

- Nurture your family with love and intention, providing a firm foundation for your children.

- Practice self-care and remain confident, radiant, and joyful.

FINAL THOUGHTS

This journal is a sacred space for you to grow in faith, take care of yourself, and embrace your journey as a mother. Stay consistent, remain intentional, and rely on God's strength every day.

The Royal Eagle Mom Journal is your guide to a stronger faith, a balanced life, and a confident spirit.

Start your journey today!

ROYAL EAGLE MOM

STATEMENT

Who is an **Eagle Mom**? An Eagle Mom is poised, graceful, and strong. She nurtures her children with both *Tough Love & Care and Tender Love & Care* (TLC x2) while staying grounded in her faith. She fights her battles through prayer and relies on Jesus in all aspects of life. This journal planner is designed to help you embody the **Eagle Mom mentality** and live a life of faith, love, and self-care. She is intentional in keeping a solid structure and foundation for a godly home and is still able to have fun with her family!

ROYAL EAGLE MOM
GOALS

PROFESSIONAL / FINANCIAL

- ○ _____
- ○ _____
- ○ _____
- ○ _____
- ○ _____
- ○ _____

VACATION

- ○ _____
- ○ _____
- ○ _____
- ○ _____
- ○ _____
- ○ _____

PERSONAL

- ○ _____
- ○ _____
- ○ _____
- ○ _____
- ○ _____
- ○ _____

FAITH / SPIRITUAL

- ○ _____
- ○ _____
- ○ _____
- ○ _____
- ○ _____
- ○ _____

PARENTING

- ○ _____
- ○ _____
- ○ _____
- ○ _____
- ○ _____
- ○ _____

PASSION – DATE

- ○ _____
- ○ _____
- ○ _____
- ○ _____
- ○ _____
- ○ _____

MONTHLY BUDGET

Keep track of your monthly bills and their due dates. As well as subscriptions and groceries.

MONTH _____

BILLS TRACKER

BILL / SUBSCRIPTION	DESCRIPTION	DUE DATE	PAID
_____	_____	_____	_____
_____	_____	_____	_____
_____	_____	_____	_____
_____	_____	_____	_____
_____	_____	_____	_____
_____	_____	_____	_____
_____	_____	_____	_____
_____	_____	_____	_____
_____	_____	_____	_____
_____	_____	_____	_____
_____	_____	_____	_____
_____	_____	_____	_____

GROCERIES

_____

_____

_____

_____

_____

REMINDERS

_____

_____

_____

_____

_____

MONTH _____

BILLS TRACKER

BILL / SUBSCRIPTION	DESCRIPTION	DUE DATE	PAID
_____	_____	_____	____
_____	_____	_____	____
_____	_____	_____	____
_____	_____	_____	____
_____	_____	_____	____
_____	_____	_____	____
_____	_____	_____	____
_____	_____	_____	____
_____	_____	_____	____
_____	_____	_____	____
_____	_____	_____	____
_____	_____	_____	____
_____	_____	_____	____

GROCERIES

_____
_____
_____
_____
_____
_____

REMINDERS

_____
_____
_____
_____
_____
_____

MONTH _____

BILLS TRACKER

BILL / SUBSCRIPTION	DESCRIPTION	DUE DATE	PAID

GROCERIES

REMINDERS

MONTH _____

BILLS TRACKER

BILL / SUBSCRIPTION	DESCRIPTION	DUE DATE	PAID
_____	_____	_____	_____
_____	_____	_____	_____
_____	_____	_____	_____
_____	_____	_____	_____
_____	_____	_____	_____
_____	_____	_____	_____
_____	_____	_____	_____
_____	_____	_____	_____
_____	_____	_____	_____
_____	_____	_____	_____
_____	_____	_____	_____
_____	_____	_____	_____
_____	_____	_____	_____

GROCERIES	REMINDERS
_____	_____
_____	_____
_____	_____
_____	_____
_____	_____
_____	_____

MONTH _____

BILLS TRACKER

BILL / SUBSCRIPTION	DESCRIPTION	DUE DATE	PAID

GROCERIES

REMINDERS

MONTH _____

BILLS TRACKER

BILL / SUBSCRIPTION	DESCRIPTION	DUE DATE	PAID

GROCERIES | REMINDERS

GROCERIES	REMINDERS

MONTH _____

BILLS TRACKER

BILL / SUBSCRIPTION	DESCRIPTION	DUE DATE	PAID
_____	_____	_____	_____
_____	_____	_____	_____
_____	_____	_____	_____
_____	_____	_____	_____
_____	_____	_____	_____
_____	_____	_____	_____
_____	_____	_____	_____
_____	_____	_____	_____
_____	_____	_____	_____
_____	_____	_____	_____
_____	_____	_____	_____
_____	_____	_____	_____

GROCERIES	REMINDERS
_____	_____
_____	_____
_____	_____
_____	_____
_____	_____
_____	_____

MONTH _____

BILLS TRACKER

BILL / SUBSCRIPTION	DESCRIPTION	DUE DATE	PAID
_____	_____	_____	_____
_____	_____	_____	_____
_____	_____	_____	_____
_____	_____	_____	_____
_____	_____	_____	_____
_____	_____	_____	_____
_____	_____	_____	_____
_____	_____	_____	_____
_____	_____	_____	_____
_____	_____	_____	_____
_____	_____	_____	_____
_____	_____	_____	_____

GROCERIES	REMINDERS
_____	_____
_____	_____
_____	_____
_____	_____
_____	_____
_____	_____

MONTH _____

BILLS TRACKER

BILL / SUBSCRIPTION	DESCRIPTION	DUE DATE	PAID

GROCERIES

REMINDERS

MONTH _____

BILLS TRACKER

BILL / SUBSCRIPTION	DESCRIPTION	DUE DATE	PAID
_____	_____	_____	_____
_____	_____	_____	_____
_____	_____	_____	_____
_____	_____	_____	_____
_____	_____	_____	_____
_____	_____	_____	_____
_____	_____	_____	_____
_____	_____	_____	_____
_____	_____	_____	_____
_____	_____	_____	_____
_____	_____	_____	_____
_____	_____	_____	_____
_____	_____	_____	_____

GROCERIES	REMINDERS
_____	_____
_____	_____
_____	_____
_____	_____
_____	_____
_____	_____

MONTH _____

BILLS TRACKER

BILL / SUBSCRIPTION	DESCRIPTION	DUE DATE	PAID

GROCERIES

REMINDERS

MONTH _____

BILLS TRACKER

BILL / SUBSCRIPTION	DESCRIPTION	DUE DATE	PAID
_____	_____	_____	_____
_____	_____	_____	_____
_____	_____	_____	_____
_____	_____	_____	_____
_____	_____	_____	_____
_____	_____	_____	_____
_____	_____	_____	_____
_____	_____	_____	_____
_____	_____	_____	_____
_____	_____	_____	_____
_____	_____	_____	_____
_____	_____	_____	_____

GROCERIES

_____

_____

_____

_____

_____

_____

REMINDERS

_____

_____

_____

_____

_____

_____

MONTH _____

BILLS TRACKER

BILL / SUBSCRIPTION	DESCRIPTION	DUE DATE	PAID
_____	_____	_____	_____
_____	_____	_____	_____
_____	_____	_____	_____
_____	_____	_____	_____
_____	_____	_____	_____
_____	_____	_____	_____
_____	_____	_____	_____
_____	_____	_____	_____
_____	_____	_____	_____
_____	_____	_____	_____
_____	_____	_____	_____
_____	_____	_____	_____

GROCERIES   REMINDERS

GROCERIES	REMINDERS
_____	_____
_____	_____
_____	_____
_____	_____
_____	_____
_____	_____

WEEKLY JOURNAL

THE 4 W's WAKE ROUTINE

WAKE EARLY

Go to bed early so you can wake up early before your family. This will allow you to have spiritual time alone, set the tone for your day, and start with prayer. Record the time you wake up each morning and note what works best for you.

WORSHIP

Read your Bible, pray, and listen for God's guidance. Memorize and meditate on a scripture verse each day. Write down the scripture that speaks to you and how it applies to your life.

WORK OUT

Move your body, whether it's stretching, walking, or a full workout session. Physical health is vital for maintaining strength and energy. Record your daily exercise routine and duration.

WATER

Start your morning with a full glass or bottle of water. Hydration is essential, and many mothers neglect this simple yet important habit. Track your daily water intake.

SELF-CARE MORNING ROUTINE

- Take a soothing shower with beautifully scented soaps and moisturize your skin.
- Dress up in something cute (even if it's casual) to boost confidence.
- Make up your bed and tidy your room to create a peaceful environment.
- Eat a light, nutritious breakfast to fuel your energy for the day.

PRAY & HUSTLE, HUSTLE & PRAY DAYTIME ROUTINE

Whether you are working, running a business, or a stay-at-home mom, cover your responsibilities in prayer. Stay humble, work diligently, and trust God to guide your steps.

- Be thankful for your job and income.
- Tithe, save, and practice financial wisdom.
- If you dislike your job, pray for better opportunities while staying grateful for your current one.
- If you are self-employed, pray for stability, growth, and longevity.
- If you are a homemaker, remember that managing a home is a sacred responsibility. Pray over your family and household.

S.L.E.E.P BEDTIME ROUTINE

S – **S**leep and Stay Calm
L – **L**ive Life in Love and Laughter
E – **E**at Healthy
E – **E**xercise Regularly
P – **P**ause and Pray!

End your day by preparing a hearty dinner, enjoying family time, and reflecting on your blessings. Write down one thing you are grateful for each night.

WORKOUT PLAN IDEAS

5–10 min speed walk or run using treadmill or running in place

50 crunches

50 jumping jacks

30 sec planks

20 squats

20 back flaps

15 sit-ups

* This is a 30–35 min. workout which can be accomplished with or without equipment; with or without your children; it can be incorporated during any time of the day and anywhere. Many times, I find myself doing some of these activities while I'm making breakfast.

STAYING ACTIVE WITH KIDS IN TOW

- Ms. Linky's Princess School (YouTube)
- YMCA Membership Activities and Classes
- Dance Party or Swim
- Stroller Walks or Jogging
- Yoga or Stretching Together
- Simon Says, But Make It Fitness Moves

MEAL IDEAS

Sunday, Tuesday and Thursday: Prepare fresh foods

- Stuffed spinach chicken and Rice
- Spaghetti and meatballs
- Fish and chips
- Beef stew
- Shrimp alfredo
- Mac and cheese grilled chicken
- Sandwiches or paninis

Monday and Wednesday: Leftovers	• Incorporate soup and dessert
	• Frozen pizza or dinner
	• Order pizza or takeout
Friday and Saturday: Takeout or another fun option	• Fun breakfast for dinner
	• Allow kids to choose and help prep even if it's messy
	• Casual or fancy restaurant

ACTIVITY IDEAS

- Create a Family Mantra or Flag
- Movie and Ice Cream Night (Theater or Home)
- Arcade
- Park
- Bike Riding
- Trampoline Park
- Splash Park
- Game Night
- Visit Botanical Gardens
- Karaoke

HAPPY THOUGHT

In life, sometimes it's the small things that count and bring a smile to our faces—the moments of laughter when our husband tickles us or when our children do or say something silly. Even a fun moment with friends encourages happiness. In this section, jot down something that made you happy during the week or use it as a space to jot down something you are grateful for. I love to think about the movie *Pollyanna*, whose "Glad Game" encourages you to find something to be glad about.

MONTH _____

	MONDAY	TUESDAY	WEDNESDAY	THURSDAY
4 W's WAKE ROUTINE	□ WAKE (TIME)	□ WAKE (TIME)	□ WAKE (TIME)	□ WAKE (TIME)
	□ WORSHIP	□ WORSHIP	□ WORSHIP	□ WORSHIP
	□ WORKOUT (TIME)	□ WORKOUT (TIME)	□ WORKOUT (TIME)	□ WORKOUT (TIME)
	□ WATER (#BOTTLES)	□ WATER (#BOTTLES)	□ WATER (#BOTTLES)	□ WATER (#BOTTLES)
SELF-CARE MORNING ROUTINE	□ SHOWER / BRUSH TEETH	□ SHOWER / BRUSH TEETH	□ SHOWER / BRUSH TEETH	□ SHOWER / BRUSH TEETH
	□ DRESS / HAIR CHECK	□ DRESS / HAIR CHECK	□ DRESS / HAIR CHECK	□ DRESS / HAIR CHECK
	□ MAKE BED / TIDY ROOM	□ MAKE BED / TIDY ROOM	□ MAKE BED / TIDY ROOM	□ MAKE BED / TIDY ROOM
	□ BREAKFAST	□ BREAKFAST	□ BREAKFAST	□ BREAKFAST
TIME	6 AM	6 AM	6 AM	6 AM
	7 AM	7 AM	7 AM	7 AM
	8 AM	8 AM	8 AM	8 AM
	9 AM	9 AM	9 AM	9 AM
	10 AM	10 AM	10 AM	10 AM
	11 AM	11 AM	11 AM	11 AM
	12 PM	12 PM	12 PM	12 PM
	1 PM	1 PM	1 PM	1 PM
	2 PM	2 PM	2 PM	2 PM
	3 PM	3 PM	3 PM	3 PM
	4 PM	4 PM	4 PM	4 PM
	5 PM	5 PM	5 PM	5 PM
	6 PM	6 PM	6 PM	6 PM
	7 PM	7 PM	7 PM	7 PM
	8 PM	8 PM	8 PM	8 PM
	9 PM	9 PM	9 PM	9 PM
	10 PM	10 PM	10P M	10 PM
	11 PM	11 PM	11 PM	11 PM
	12 AM	12 AM	12 AM	12 AM
	MEAL	**MEAL**	**MEAL**	**MEAL**

S.L.E.E.P BEDTIME ROUTINE

ACTIVITIES FOR THE WEEK

BIBLE VERSE OF THE WEEK _____

FRIDAY	SATURDAY	SUNDAY

PRAY & HUSTLE, HUSTLE & PRAY DAYTIME ROUTINE

FRIDAY	SATURDAY	SUNDAY
☐ WAKE (TIME)	☐ WAKE (TIME)	☐ WAKE (TIME)
☐ WORSHIP	☐ WORSHIP	☐ WORSHIP
☐ WORKOUT (TIME)	☐ WORKOUT (TIME)	☐ WORKOUT (TIME)
☐ WATER (#BOTTLES)	☐ WATER (#BOTTLES)	☐ WATER (#BOTTLES)
☐ SHOWER / BRUSH TEETH	☐ SHOWER / BRUSH TEETH	☐ SHOWER / BRUSH TEETH
☐ DRESS / HAIR CHECK	☐ DRESS / HAIR CHECK	☐ DRESS / HAIR CHECK
☐ MAKE BED / TIDY ROOM	☐ MAKE BED / TIDY ROOM	☐ MAKE BED / TIDY ROOM
☐ BREAKFAST	☐ BREAKFAST	☐ BREAKFAST

FRIDAY	SATURDAY	SUNDAY
6 AM	6 AM	6 AM
7 AM	7 AM	7 AM
8 AM	8 AM	8 AM
9 AM	9 AM	9 AM
10 AM	10 AM	10 AM
11 AM	11 AM	11 AM
12 PM	12 PM	12 PM
1 PM	1 PM	1 PM
2 PM	2 PM	2 PM
3 PM	3 PM	3 PM
4 PM	4 PM	4 PM
5 PM	5 PM	5 PM
6 PM	6 PM	6 PM
7 PM	7 PM	7 PM
8 PM	8 PM	8 PM
9 PM	9 PM	9 PM
10 PM	10 PM	10 PM
11 PM	11 PM	11 PM
12 AM	12 AM	12 AM

REMINDERS / NOTES

MEAL	MEAL	MEAL

S.L.E.E.P BEDTIME ROUTINE

HAPPY THOUGHTS

ACTIVITIES FOR THE WEEK

	MONDAY	TUESDAY	WEDNESDAY	THURSDAY
4 W's WAKE ROUTINE	☐ WAKE (TIME) ☐ WORSHIP ☐ WORKOUT (TIME) ☐ WATER (#BOTTLES)	☐ WAKE (TIME) ☐ WORSHIP ☐ WORKOUT (TIME) ☐ WATER (#BOTTLES)	☐ WAKE (TIME) ☐ WORSHIP ☐ WORKOUT (TIME) ☐ WATER (#BOTTLES)	☐ WAKE (TIME) ☐ WORSHIP ☐ WORKOUT (TIME) ☐ WATER (#BOTTLES)
SELF-CARE MORNING ROUTINE	☐ SHOWER / BRUSH TEETH ☐ DRESS / HAIR CHECK ☐ MAKE BED / TIDY ROOM ☐ BREAKFAST	☐ SHOWER / BRUSH TEETH ☐ DRESS / HAIR CHECK ☐ MAKE BED / TIDY ROOM ☐ BREAKFAST	☐ SHOWER / BRUSH TEETH ☐ DRESS / HAIR CHECK ☐ MAKE BED / TIDY ROOM ☐ BREAKFAST	☐ SHOWER / BRUSH TEETH ☐ DRESS / HAIR CHECK ☐ MAKE BED / TIDY ROOM ☐ BREAKFAST
TIME	6 AM 7 AM 8 AM 9 AM 10 AM 11 AM 12 PM 1 PM 2 PM 3 PM 4 PM 5 PM 6 PM 7 PM 8 PM 9 PM 10 PM 11 PM 12 AM	6 AM 7 AM 8 AM 9 AM 10 AM 11 AM 12 PM 1 PM 2 PM 3 PM 4 PM 5 PM 6 PM 7 PM 8 PM 9 PM 10 PM 11 PM 12 AM	6 AM 7 AM 8 AM 9 AM 10 AM 11 AM 12 PM 1 PM 2 PM 3 PM 4 PM 5 PM 6 PM 7 PM 8 PM 9 PM 10P M 11 PM 12 AM	6 AM 7 AM 8 AM 9 AM 10 AM 11 AM 12 PM 1 PM 2 PM 3 PM 4 PM 5 PM 6 PM 7 PM 8 PM 9 PM 10 PM 11 PM 12 AM

MEAL	MEAL	MEAL	MEAL
_____	_____	_____	_____

S.L.E.E.P BEDTIME ROUTINE

_____	_____	_____	_____
_____	_____	_____	_____

ACTIVITIES FOR THE WEEK

_____	_____	_____	_____

FRIDAY	SATURDAY	SUNDAY
☐ WAKE (TIME)	☐ WAKE (TIME)	☐ WAKE (TIME)
☐ WORSHIP	☐ WORSHIP	☐ WORSHIP
☐ WORKOUT (TIME)	☐ WORKOUT (TIME)	☐ WORKOUT (TIME)
☐ WATER (#BOTTLES)	☐ WATER (#BOTTLES)	☐ WATER (#BOTTLES)
☐ SHOWER / BRUSH TEETH	☐ SHOWER / BRUSH TEETH	☐ SHOWER / BRUSH TEETH
☐ DRESS / HAIR CHECK	☐ DRESS / HAIR CHECK	☐ DRESS / HAIR CHECK
☐ MAKE BED / TIDY ROOM	☐ MAKE BED / TIDY ROOM	☐ MAKE BED / TIDY ROOM
☐ BREAKFAST	☐ BREAKFAST	☐ BREAKFAST

PRAY & HUSTLE, HUSTLE & PRAY DAYTIME ROUTINE

FRIDAY	SATURDAY	SUNDAY
6 AM	6 AM	6 AM
7 AM	7 AM	7 AM
8 AM	8 AM	8 AM
9 AM	9 AM	9 AM
10 AM	10 AM	10 AM
11 AM	11 AM	11 AM
12 PM	12 PM	12 PM
1 PM	1 PM	1 PM
2 PM	2 PM	2 PM
3 PM	3 PM	3 PM
4 PM	4 PM	4 PM
5 PM	5 PM	5 PM
6 PM	6 PM	6 PM
7 PM	7 PM	7 PM
8 PM	8 PM	8 PM
9 PM	9 PM	9 PM
10 PM	10 PM	10 PM
11 PM	11 PM	11 PM
12 AM	12 AM	12 AM

REMINDERS / NOTES

MEAL	MEAL	MEAL

S.L.E.E.P BEDTIME ROUTINE

HAPPY THOUGHTS

ACTIVITIES FOR THE WEEK

	MONDAY	TUESDAY	WEDNESDAY	THURSDAY
4 W's WAKE ROUTINE	☐ WAKE (TIME) ☐ WORSHIP ☐ WORKOUT (TIME) ☐ WATER (#BOTTLES)	☐ WAKE (TIME) ☐ WORSHIP ☐ WORKOUT (TIME) ☐ WATER (#BOTTLES)	☐ WAKE (TIME) ☐ WORSHIP ☐ WORKOUT (TIME) ☐ WATER (#BOTTLES)	☐ WAKE (TIME) ☐ WORSHIP ☐ WORKOUT (TIME) ☐ WATER (#BOTTLES)
SELF-CARE MORNING ROUTINE	☐ SHOWER / BRUSH TEETH ☐ DRESS / HAIR CHECK ☐ MAKE BED / TIDY ROOM ☐ BREAKFAST	☐ SHOWER / BRUSH TEETH ☐ DRESS / HAIR CHECK ☐ MAKE BED / TIDY ROOM ☐ BREAKFAST	☐ SHOWER / BRUSH TEETH ☐ DRESS / HAIR CHECK ☐ MAKE BED / TIDY ROOM ☐ BREAKFAST	☐ SHOWER / BRUSH TEETH ☐ DRESS / HAIR CHECK ☐ MAKE BED / TIDY ROOM ☐ BREAKFAST
TIME	6 AM 7 AM 8 AM 9 AM 10 AM 11 AM 12 PM 1 PM 2 PM 3 PM 4 PM 5 PM 6 PM 7 PM 8 PM 9 PM 10 PM 11 PM 12 AM	6 AM 7 AM 8 AM 9 AM 10 AM 11 AM 12 PM 1 PM 2 PM 3 PM 4 PM 5 PM 6 PM 7 PM 8 PM 9 PM 10 PM 11 PM 12 AM	6 AM 7 AM 8 AM 9 AM 10 AM 11 AM 12 PM 1 PM 2 PM 3 PM 4 PM 5 PM 6 PM 7 PM 8 PM 9 PM 10P M 11 PM 12 AM	6 AM 7 AM 8 AM 9 AM 10 AM 11 AM 12 PM 1 PM 2 PM 3 PM 4 PM 5 PM 6 PM 7 PM 8 PM 9 PM 10 PM 11 PM 12 AM
	MEAL	MEAL	MEAL	MEAL

S.L.E.E.P BEDTIME ROUTINE

ACTIVITIES FOR THE WEEK

BIBLE VERSE OF THE WEEK _____

FRIDAY	SATURDAY	SUNDAY

PRAY & HUSTLE, HUSTLE & PRAY DAYTIME ROUTINE

FRIDAY	SATURDAY	SUNDAY
☐ WAKE (TIME)	☐ WAKE (TIME)	☐ WAKE (TIME)
☐ WORSHIP	☐ WORSHIP	☐ WORSHIP
☐ WORKOUT (TIME)	☐ WORKOUT (TIME)	☐ WORKOUT (TIME)
☐ WATER (#BOTTLES)	☐ WATER (#BOTTLES)	☐ WATER (#BOTTLES)
☐ SHOWER / BRUSH TEETH	☐ SHOWER / BRUSH TEETH	☐ SHOWER / BRUSH TEETH
☐ DRESS / HAIR CHECK	☐ DRESS / HAIR CHECK	☐ DRESS / HAIR CHECK
☐ MAKE BED / TIDY ROOM	☐ MAKE BED / TIDY ROOM	☐ MAKE BED / TIDY ROOM
☐ BREAKFAST	☐ BREAKFAST	☐ BREAKFAST

6 AM	6 AM	6 AM
7 AM	7 AM	7 AM
8 AM	8 AM	8 AM
9 AM	9 AM	9 AM
10 AM	10 AM	10 AM
11 AM	11 AM	11 AM
12 PM	12 PM	12 PM
1 PM	1 PM	1 PM
2 PM	2 PM	2 PM
3 PM	3 PM	3 PM
4 PM	4 PM	4 PM
5 PM	5 PM	5 PM
6 PM	6 PM	6 PM
7 PM	7 PM	7 PM
8 PM	8 PM	8 PM
9 PM	9 PM	9 PM
10 PM	10 PM	10 PM
11 PM	11 PM	11 PM
12 AM	12 AM	12 AM

REMINDERS / NOTES

MEAL	MEAL	MEAL

S.L.E.E.P BEDTIME ROUTINE

ACTIVITIES FOR THE WEEK

HAPPY THOUGHTS

	MONTH		

	MONDAY	TUESDAY	WEDNESDAY	THURSDAY
4 W's WAKE ROUTINE	☐ WAKE (TIME) ☐ WORSHIP ☐ WORKOUT (TIME) ☐ WATER (#BOTTLES)	☐ WAKE (TIME) ☐ WORSHIP ☐ WORKOUT (TIME) ☐ WATER (#BOTTLES)	☐ WAKE (TIME) ☐ WORSHIP ☐ WORKOUT (TIME) ☐ WATER (#BOTTLES)	☐ WAKE (TIME) ☐ WORSHIP ☐ WORKOUT (TIME) ☐ WATER (#BOTTLES)
SELF-CARE MORNING ROUTINE	☐ SHOWER / BRUSH TEETH ☐ DRESS / HAIR CHECK ☐ MAKE BED / TIDY ROOM ☐ BREAKFAST	☐ SHOWER / BRUSH TEETH ☐ DRESS / HAIR CHECK ☐ MAKE BED / TIDY ROOM ☐ BREAKFAST	☐ SHOWER / BRUSH TEETH ☐ DRESS / HAIR CHECK ☐ MAKE BED / TIDY ROOM ☐ BREAKFAST	☐ SHOWER / BRUSH TEETH ☐ DRESS / HAIR CHECK ☐ MAKE BED / TIDY ROOM ☐ BREAKFAST
TIME	6 AM 7 AM 8 AM 9 AM 10 AM 11 AM 12 PM 1 PM 2 PM 3 PM 4 PM 5 PM 6 PM 7 PM 8 PM 9 PM 10 PM 11 PM 12 AM	6 AM 7 AM 8 AM 9 AM 10 AM 11 AM 12 PM 1 PM 2 PM 3 PM 4 PM 5 PM 6 PM 7 PM 8 PM 9 PM 10 PM 11 PM 12 AM	6 AM 7 AM 8 AM 9 AM 10 AM 11 AM 12 PM 1 PM 2 PM 3 PM 4 PM 5 PM 6 PM 7 PM 8 PM 9 PM 10P M 11 PM 12 AM	6 AM 7 AM 8 AM 9 AM 10 AM 11 AM 12 PM 1 PM 2 PM 3 PM 4 PM 5 PM 6 PM 7 PM 8 PM 9 PM 10 PM 11 PM 12 AM
	MEAL	**MEAL**	**MEAL**	**MEAL**

S.L.E.E.P BEDTIME ROUTINE

ACTIVITIES FOR THE WEEK

BIBLE VERSE OF THE WEEK _____

FRIDAY

☐ WAKE (TIME) _____
☐ WORSHIP _____
☐ WORKOUT (TIME) _____
☐ WATER (#BOTTLES) _____

☐ SHOWER / BRUSH TEETH
☐ DRESS / HAIR CHECK
☐ MAKE BED / TIDY ROOM
☐ BREAKFAST

6 AM _____
7 AM _____
8 AM _____
9 AM _____
10 AM _____
11 AM _____
12 PM _____
1 PM _____
2 PM _____
3 PM _____
4 PM _____
5 PM _____
6 PM _____
7 PM _____
8 PM _____
9 PM _____
10 PM _____
11 PM _____
12 AM _____

SATURDAY

☐ WAKE (TIME) _____
☐ WORSHIP _____
☐ WORKOUT (TIME) _____
☐ WATER (#BOTTLES) _____

☐ SHOWER / BRUSH TEETH
☐ DRESS / HAIR CHECK
☐ MAKE BED / TIDY ROOM
☐ BREAKFAST

6 AM _____
7 AM _____
8 AM _____
9 AM _____
10 AM _____
11 AM _____
12 PM _____
1 PM _____
2 PM _____
3 PM _____
4 PM _____
5 PM _____
6 PM _____
7 PM _____
8 PM _____
9 PM _____
10 PM _____
11 PM _____
12 AM _____

SUNDAY

☐ WAKE (TIME) _____
☐ WORSHIP _____
☐ WORKOUT (TIME) _____
☐ WATER (#BOTTLES) _____

☐ SHOWER / BRUSH TEETH
☐ DRESS / HAIR CHECK
☐ MAKE BED / TIDY ROOM
☐ BREAKFAST

6 AM _____
7 AM _____
8 AM _____
9 AM _____
10 AM _____
11 AM _____
12 PM _____
1 PM _____
2 PM _____
3 PM _____
4 PM _____
5 PM _____
6 PM _____
7 PM _____
8 PM _____
9 PM _____
10 PM _____
11 PM _____
12 AM _____

PRAY & HUSTLE, HUSTLE & PRAY DAYTIME ROUTINE

_____

_____

_____

REMINDERS / NOTES

_____

_____

_____

_____

_____

HAPPY THOUGHTS

_____
_____
_____
_____
_____

MEAL _____   MEAL _____   MEAL _____

_____   _____   _____

S.L.E.E.P BEDTIME ROUTINE

_____   _____   _____

_____   _____   _____

ACTIVITIES FOR THE WEEK

_____   _____   _____

	MONDAY	TUESDAY	WEDNESDAY	THURSDAY
4 W's WAKE ROUTINE	□ WAKE (TIME) □ WORSHIP □ WORKOUT (TIME) □ WATER (#BOTTLES)	□ WAKE (TIME) □ WORSHIP □ WORKOUT (TIME) □ WATER (#BOTTLES)	□ WAKE (TIME) □ WORSHIP □ WORKOUT (TIME) □ WATER (#BOTTLES)	□ WAKE (TIME) □ WORSHIP □ WORKOUT (TIME) □ WATER (#BOTTLES)
SELF-CARE MORNING ROUTINE	□ SHOWER / BRUSH TEETH □ DRESS / HAIR CHECK □ MAKE BED / TIDY ROOM □ BREAKFAST	□ SHOWER / BRUSH TEETH □ DRESS / HAIR CHECK □ MAKE BED / TIDY ROOM □ BREAKFAST	□ SHOWER / BRUSH TEETH □ DRESS / HAIR CHECK □ MAKE BED / TIDY ROOM □ BREAKFAST	□ SHOWER / BRUSH TEETH □ DRESS / HAIR CHECK □ MAKE BED / TIDY ROOM □ BREAKFAST
TIME	6 AM 7 AM 8 AM 9 AM 10 AM 11 AM 12 PM 1 PM 2 PM 3 PM 4 PM 5 PM 6 PM 7 PM 8 PM 9 PM 10 PM 11 PM 12 AM	6 AM 7 AM 8 AM 9 AM 10 AM 11 AM 12 PM 1 PM 2 PM 3 PM 4 PM 5 PM 6 PM 7 PM 8 PM 9 PM 10 PM 11 PM 12 AM	6 AM 7 AM 8 AM 9 AM 10 AM 11 AM 12 PM 1 PM 2 PM 3 PM 4 PM 5 PM 6 PM 7 PM 8 PM 9 PM 10P M 11 PM 12 AM	6 AM 7 AM 8 AM 9 AM 10 AM 11 AM 12 PM 1 PM 2 PM 3 PM 4 PM 5 PM 6 PM 7 PM 8 PM 9 PM 10 PM 11 PM 12 AM
	MEAL	MEAL	MEAL	MEAL

MONTH _____

S.L.E.E.P BEDTIME ROUTINE

ACTIVITIES FOR THE WEEK

BIBLE VERSE OF THE WEEK _____

FRIDAY

☐ WAKE (TIME) _____
☐ WORSHIP _____
☐ WORKOUT (TIME) _____
☐ WATER (#BOTTLES) _____

☐ SHOWER / BRUSH TEETH
☐ DRESS / HAIR CHECK
☐ MAKE BED / TIDY ROOM
☐ BREAKFAST

6 AM _____
7 AM _____
8 AM _____
9 AM _____
10 AM _____
11 AM _____
12 PM _____
1 PM _____
2 PM _____
3 PM _____
4 PM _____
5 PM _____
6 PM _____
7 PM _____
8 PM _____
9 PM _____
10 PM _____
11 PM _____
12 AM _____

MEAL _____

SATURDAY

☐ WAKE (TIME) _____
☐ WORSHIP _____
☐ WORKOUT (TIME) _____
☐ WATER (#BOTTLES) _____

☐ SHOWER / BRUSH TEETH
☐ DRESS / HAIR CHECK
☐ MAKE BED / TIDY ROOM
☐ BREAKFAST

6 AM _____
7 AM _____
8 AM _____
9 AM _____
10 AM _____
11 AM _____
12 PM _____
1 PM _____
2 PM _____
3 PM _____
4 PM _____
5 PM _____
6 PM _____
7 PM _____
8 PM _____
9 PM _____
10 PM _____
11 PM _____
12 AM _____

MEAL _____

S.L.E.E.P BEDTIME ROUTINE

SUNDAY

☐ WAKE (TIME) _____
☐ WORSHIP _____
☐ WORKOUT (TIME) _____
☐ WATER (#BOTTLES) _____

☐ SHOWER / BRUSH TEETH
☐ DRESS / HAIR CHECK
☐ MAKE BED / TIDY ROOM
☐ BREAKFAST

6 AM _____
7 AM _____
8 AM _____
9 AM _____
10 AM _____
11 AM _____
12 PM _____
1 PM _____
2 PM _____
3 PM _____
4 PM _____
5 PM _____
6 PM _____
7 PM _____
8 PM _____
9 PM _____
10 PM _____
11 PM _____
12 AM _____

MEAL _____

ACTIVITIES FOR THE WEEK

PRAY & HUSTLE, HUSTLE & PRAY DAYTIME ROUTINE

REMINDERS / NOTES

HAPPY THOUGHTS

	MONDAY	TUESDAY	WEDNESDAY	THURSDAY
MONTH				

4 W's WAKE ROUTINE	☐ WAKE (TIME)	☐ WAKE (TIME)	☐ WAKE (TIME)	☐ WAKE (TIME)
	☐ WORSHIP	☐ WORSHIP	☐ WORSHIP	☐ WORSHIP
	☐ WORKOUT (TIME)	☐ WORKOUT (TIME)	☐ WORKOUT (TIME)	☐ WORKOUT (TIME)
	☐ WATER (#BOTTLES)	☐ WATER (#BOTTLES)	☐ WATER (#BOTTLES)	☐ WATER (#BOTTLES)
SELF-CARE MORNING ROUTINE	☐ SHOWER / BRUSH TEETH	☐ SHOWER / BRUSH TEETH	☐ SHOWER / BRUSH TEETH	☐ SHOWER / BRUSH TEETH
	☐ DRESS / HAIR CHECK	☐ DRESS / HAIR CHECK	☐ DRESS / HAIR CHECK	☐ DRESS / HAIR CHECK
	☐ MAKE BED / TIDY ROOM	☐ MAKE BED / TIDY ROOM	☐ MAKE BED / TIDY ROOM	☐ MAKE BED / TIDY ROOM
	☐ BREAKFAST	☐ BREAKFAST	☐ BREAKFAST	☐ BREAKFAST

TIME				
6 AM	6 AM	6 AM	6 AM
7 AM	7 AM	7 AM	7 AM
8 AM	8 AM	8 AM	8 AM
9 AM	9 AM	9 AM	9 AM
10 AM	10 AM	10 AM	10 AM
11 AM	11 AM	11 AM	11 AM
12 PM	12 PM	12 PM	12 PM
1 PM	1 PM	1 PM	1 PM
2 PM	2 PM	2 PM	2 PM
3 PM	3 PM	3 PM	3 PM
4 PM	4 PM	4 PM	4 PM
5 PM	5 PM	5 PM	5 PM
6 PM	6 PM	6 PM	6 PM
7 PM	7 PM	7 PM	7 PM
8 PM	8 PM	8 PM	8 PM
9 PM	9 PM	9 PM	9 PM
10 PM	10 PM	10P M	10 PM
11 PM	11 PM	11 PM	11 PM
12 AM	12 AM	12 AM	12 AM

MEAL	MEAL	MEAL	MEAL

S.L.E.E.P BEDTIME ROUTINE

ACTIVITIES FOR THE WEEK

BIBLE VERSE OF THE WEEK _____

FRIDAY

☐ WAKE (TIME) _____
☐ WORSHIP _____
☐ WORKOUT (TIME) _____
☐ WATER (#BOTTLES) _____

☐ SHOWER / BRUSH TEETH
☐ DRESS / HAIR CHECK
☐ MAKE BED / TIDY ROOM
☐ BREAKFAST

6 AM _____
7 AM _____
8 AM _____
9 AM _____
10 AM _____
11 AM _____
12 PM _____
1 PM _____
2 PM _____
3 PM _____
4 PM _____
5 PM _____
6 PM _____
7 PM _____
8 PM _____
9 PM _____
10 PM _____
11 PM _____
12 AM _____

MEAL

_____

SATURDAY

☐ WAKE (TIME) _____
☐ WORSHIP _____
☐ WORKOUT (TIME) _____
☐ WATER (#BOTTLES) _____

☐ SHOWER / BRUSH TEETH
☐ DRESS / HAIR CHECK
☐ MAKE BED / TIDY ROOM
☐ BREAKFAST

6 AM _____
7 AM _____
8 AM _____
9 AM _____
10 AM _____
11 AM _____
12 PM _____
1 PM _____
2 PM _____
3 PM _____
4 PM _____
5 PM _____
6 PM _____
7 PM _____
8 PM _____
9 PM _____
10 PM _____
11 PM _____
12 AM _____

MEAL

S.L.E.E.P BEDTIME ROUTINE

_____

ACTIVITIES FOR THE WEEK

_____

SUNDAY

☐ WAKE (TIME) _____
☐ WORSHIP _____
☐ WORKOUT (TIME) _____
☐ WATER (#BOTTLES) _____

☐ SHOWER / BRUSH TEETH
☐ DRESS / HAIR CHECK
☐ MAKE BED / TIDY ROOM
☐ BREAKFAST

6 AM _____
7 AM _____
8 AM _____
9 AM _____
10 AM _____
11 AM _____
12 PM _____
1 PM _____
2 PM _____
3 PM _____
4 PM _____
5 PM _____
6 PM _____
7 PM _____
8 PM _____
9 PM _____
10 PM _____
11 PM _____
12 AM _____

MEAL

_____

PRAY & HUSTLE, HUSTLE & PRAY DAYTIME ROUTINE

_____

REMINDERS / NOTES

_____

HAPPY THOUGHTS

_____

	MONDAY	TUESDAY	WEDNESDAY	THURSDAY
4 W's WAKE ROUTINE	☐ WAKE (TIME) ☐ WORSHIP ☐ WORKOUT (TIME) ☐ WATER (#BOTTLES)	☐ WAKE (TIME) ☐ WORSHIP ☐ WORKOUT (TIME) ☐ WATER (#BOTTLES)	☐ WAKE (TIME) ☐ WORSHIP ☐ WORKOUT (TIME) ☐ WATER (#BOTTLES)	☐ WAKE (TIME) ☐ WORSHIP ☐ WORKOUT (TIME) ☐ WATER (#BOTTLES)
SELF-CARE MORNING ROUTINE	☐ SHOWER / BRUSH TEETH ☐ DRESS / HAIR CHECK ☐ MAKE BED / TIDY ROOM ☐ BREAKFAST	☐ SHOWER / BRUSH TEETH ☐ DRESS / HAIR CHECK ☐ MAKE BED / TIDY ROOM ☐ BREAKFAST	☐ SHOWER / BRUSH TEETH ☐ DRESS / HAIR CHECK ☐ MAKE BED / TIDY ROOM ☐ BREAKFAST	☐ SHOWER / BRUSH TEETH ☐ DRESS / HAIR CHECK ☐ MAKE BED / TIDY ROOM ☐ BREAKFAST
TIME	6 AM 7 AM 8 AM 9 AM 10 AM 11 AM 12 PM 1 PM 2 PM 3 PM 4 PM 5 PM 6 PM 7 PM 8 PM 9 PM 10 PM 11 PM 12 AM	6 AM 7 AM 8 AM 9 AM 10 AM 11 AM 12 PM 1 PM 2 PM 3 PM 4 PM 5 PM 6 PM 7 PM 8 PM 9 PM 10 PM 11 PM 12 AM	6 AM 7 AM 8 AM 9 AM 10 AM 11 AM 12 PM 1 PM 2 PM 3 PM 4 PM 5 PM 6 PM 7 PM 8 PM 9 PM 10P M 11 PM 12 AM	6 AM 7 AM 8 AM 9 AM 10 AM 11 AM 12 PM 1 PM 2 PM 3 PM 4 PM 5 PM 6 PM 7 PM 8 PM 9 PM 10 PM 11 PM 12 AM
	MEAL	MEAL	MEAL	MEAL

S.L.E.E.P BEDTIME ROUTINE

ACTIVITIES FOR THE WEEK

BIBLE VERSE OF THE WEEK _____

FRIDAY	SATURDAY	SUNDAY
□ WAKE (TIME)	□ WAKE (TIME)	□ WAKE (TIME)
□ WORSHIP	□ WORSHIP	□ WORSHIP
□ WORKOUT (TIME)	□ WORKOUT (TIME)	□ WORKOUT (TIME)
□ WATER (#BOTTLES)	□ WATER (#BOTTLES)	□ WATER (#BOTTLES)
□ SHOWER / BRUSH TEETH	□ SHOWER / BRUSH TEETH	□ SHOWER / BRUSH TEETH
□ DRESS / HAIR CHECK	□ DRESS / HAIR CHECK	□ DRESS / HAIR CHECK
□ MAKE BED / TIDY ROOM	□ MAKE BED / TIDY ROOM	□ MAKE BED / TIDY ROOM
□ BREAKFAST	□ BREAKFAST	□ BREAKFAST

PRAY & HUSTLE, HUSTLE & PRAY DAYTIME ROUTINE

FRIDAY	SATURDAY	SUNDAY
6 AM	6 AM	6 AM
7 AM	7 AM	7 AM
8 AM	8 AM	8 AM
9 AM	9 AM	9 AM
10 AM	10 AM	10 AM
11 AM	11 AM	11 AM
12 PM	12 PM	12 PM
1 PM	1 PM	1 PM
2 PM	2 PM	2 PM
3 PM	3 PM	3 PM
4 PM	4 PM	4 PM
5 PM	5 PM	5 PM
6 PM	6 PM	6 PM
7 PM	7 PM	7 PM
8 PM	8 PM	8 PM
9 PM	9 PM	9 PM
10 PM	10 PM	10 PM
11 PM	11 PM	11 PM
12 AM	12 AM	12 AM

REMINDERS / NOTES

MEAL	MEAL	MEAL

S.L.E.E.P BEDTIME ROUTINE

HAPPY THOUGHTS

ACTIVITIES FOR THE WEEK

MONTH _____

	MONDAY	TUESDAY	WEDNESDAY	THURSDAY
4 W's WAKE ROUTINE	☐ WAKE (TIME) ☐ WORSHIP ☐ WORKOUT (TIME) ☐ WATER (#BOTTLES)	☐ WAKE (TIME) ☐ WORSHIP ☐ WORKOUT (TIME) ☐ WATER (#BOTTLES)	☐ WAKE (TIME) ☐ WORSHIP ☐ WORKOUT (TIME) ☐ WATER (#BOTTLES)	☐ WAKE (TIME) ☐ WORSHIP ☐ WORKOUT (TIME) ☐ WATER (#BOTTLES)
SELF-CARE MORNING ROUTINE	☐ SHOWER / BRUSH TEETH ☐ DRESS / HAIR CHECK ☐ MAKE BED / TIDY ROOM ☐ BREAKFAST	☐ SHOWER / BRUSH TEETH ☐ DRESS / HAIR CHECK ☐ MAKE BED / TIDY ROOM ☐ BREAKFAST	☐ SHOWER / BRUSH TEETH ☐ DRESS / HAIR CHECK ☐ MAKE BED / TIDY ROOM ☐ BREAKFAST	☐ SHOWER / BRUSH TEETH ☐ DRESS / HAIR CHECK ☐ MAKE BED / TIDY ROOM ☐ BREAKFAST
TIME	6 AM 7 AM 8 AM 9 AM 10 AM 11 AM 12 PM 1 PM 2 PM 3 PM 4 PM 5 PM 6 PM 7 PM 8 PM 9 PM 10 PM 11 PM 12 AM	6 AM 7 AM 8 AM 9 AM 10 AM 11 AM 12 PM 1 PM 2 PM 3 PM 4 PM 5 PM 6 PM 7 PM 8 PM 9 PM 10 PM 11 PM 12 AM	6 AM 7 AM 8 AM 9 AM 10 AM 11 AM 12 PM 1 PM 2 PM 3 PM 4 PM 5 PM 6 PM 7 PM 8 PM 9 PM 10P M 11 PM 12 AM	6 AM 7 AM 8 AM 9 AM 10 AM 11 AM 12 PM 1 PM 2 PM 3 PM 4 PM 5 PM 6 PM 7 PM 8 PM 9 PM 10 PM 11 PM 12 AM
MEAL				

S.L.E.E.P BEDTIME ROUTINE

ACTIVITIES FOR THE WEEK

BIBLE VERSE OF THE WEEK _____

FRIDAY	SATURDAY	SUNDAY
☐ WAKE (TIME)	☐ WAKE (TIME)	☐ WAKE (TIME)
☐ WORSHIP	☐ WORSHIP	☐ WORSHIP
☐ WORKOUT (TIME)	☐ WORKOUT (TIME)	☐ WORKOUT (TIME)
☐ WATER (#BOTTLES)	☐ WATER (#BOTTLES)	☐ WATER (#BOTTLES)
☐ SHOWER / BRUSH TEETH	☐ SHOWER / BRUSH TEETH	☐ SHOWER / BRUSH TEETH
☐ DRESS / HAIR CHECK	☐ DRESS / HAIR CHECK	☐ DRESS / HAIR CHECK
☐ MAKE BED / TIDY ROOM	☐ MAKE BED / TIDY ROOM	☐ MAKE BED / TIDY ROOM
☐ BREAKFAST	☐ BREAKFAST	☐ BREAKFAST

PRAY & HUSTLE, HUSTLE & PRAY DAYTIME ROUTINE

_____
_____
_____
_____
_____

FRIDAY	SATURDAY	SUNDAY
6 AM	6 AM	6 AM
7 AM	7 AM	7 AM
8 AM	8 AM	8 AM
9 AM	9 AM	9 AM
10 AM	10 AM	10 AM
11 AM	11 AM	11 AM
12 PM	12 PM	12 PM
1 PM	1 PM	1 PM
2 PM	2 PM	2 PM
3 PM	3 PM	3 PM
4 PM	4 PM	4 PM
5 PM	5 PM	5 PM
6 PM	6 PM	6 PM
7 PM	7 PM	7 PM
8 PM	8 PM	8 PM
9 PM	9 PM	9 PM
10 PM	10 PM	10 PM
11 PM	11 PM	11 PM
12 AM	12 AM	12 AM

REMINDERS / NOTES

_____
_____
_____
_____
_____

MEAL	MEAL	MEAL

S.L.E.E.P BEDTIME ROUTINE

HAPPY THOUGHTS
_____
_____
_____
_____
_____

ACTIVITIES FOR THE WEEK

_____   _____   _____

	MONTH			

	MONDAY	TUESDAY	WEDNESDAY	THURSDAY
4 W's WAKE ROUTINE	□ WAKE (TIME) □ WORSHIP □ WORKOUT (TIME) □ WATER (#BOTTLES)	□ WAKE (TIME) □ WORSHIP □ WORKOUT (TIME) □ WATER (#BOTTLES)	□ WAKE (TIME) □ WORSHIP □ WORKOUT (TIME) □ WATER (#BOTTLES)	□ WAKE (TIME) □ WORSHIP □ WORKOUT (TIME) □ WATER (#BOTTLES)
SELF-CARE MORNING ROUTINE	□ SHOWER / BRUSH TEETH □ DRESS / HAIR CHECK □ MAKE BED / TIDY ROOM □ BREAKFAST	□ SHOWER / BRUSH TEETH □ DRESS / HAIR CHECK □ MAKE BED / TIDY ROOM □ BREAKFAST	□ SHOWER / BRUSH TEETH □ DRESS / HAIR CHECK □ MAKE BED / TIDY ROOM □ BREAKFAST	□ SHOWER / BRUSH TEETH □ DRESS / HAIR CHECK □ MAKE BED / TIDY ROOM □ BREAKFAST
TIME	6 AM 7 AM 8 AM 9 AM 10 AM 11 AM 12 PM 1 PM 2 PM 3 PM 4 PM 5 PM 6 PM 7 PM 8 PM 9 PM 10 PM 11 PM 12 AM	6 AM 7 AM 8 AM 9 AM 10 AM 11 AM 12 PM 1 PM 2 PM 3 PM 4 PM 5 PM 6 PM 7 PM 8 PM 9 PM 10 PM 11 PM 12 AM	6 AM 7 AM 8 AM 9 AM 10 AM 11 AM 12 PM 1 PM 2 PM 3 PM 4 PM 5 PM 6 PM 7 PM 8 PM 9 PM 10P M 11 PM 12 AM	6 AM 7 AM 8 AM 9 AM 10 AM 11 AM 12 PM 1 PM 2 PM 3 PM 4 PM 5 PM 6 PM 7 PM 8 PM 9 PM 10 PM 11 PM 12 AM
	MEAL	MEAL	MEAL	MEAL

S.L.E.E.P BEDTIME ROUTINE

ACTIVITIES FOR THE WEEK

BIBLE VERSE OF THE WEEK _____

FRIDAY	SATURDAY	SUNDAY
☐ WAKE (TIME)	☐ WAKE (TIME)	☐ WAKE (TIME)
☐ WORSHIP	☐ WORSHIP	☐ WORSHIP
☐ WORKOUT (TIME)	☐ WORKOUT (TIME)	☐ WORKOUT (TIME)
☐ WATER (#BOTTLES)	☐ WATER (#BOTTLES)	☐ WATER (#BOTTLES)
☐ SHOWER / BRUSH TEETH	☐ SHOWER / BRUSH TEETH	☐ SHOWER / BRUSH TEETH
☐ DRESS / HAIR CHECK	☐ DRESS / HAIR CHECK	☐ DRESS / HAIR CHECK
☐ MAKE BED / TIDY ROOM	☐ MAKE BED / TIDY ROOM	☐ MAKE BED / TIDY ROOM
☐ BREAKFAST	☐ BREAKFAST	☐ BREAKFAST

PRAY & HUSTLE, HUSTLE & PRAY DAYTIME ROUTINE

FRIDAY	SATURDAY	SUNDAY
6 AM	6 AM	6 AM
7 AM	7 AM	7 AM
8 AM	8 AM	8 AM
9 AM	9 AM	9 AM
10 AM	10 AM	10 AM
11 AM	11 AM	11 AM
12 PM	12 PM	12 PM
1 PM	1 PM	1 PM
2 PM	2 PM	2 PM
3 PM	3 PM	3 PM
4 PM	4 PM	4 PM
5 PM	5 PM	5 PM
6 PM	6 PM	6 PM
7 PM	7 PM	7 PM
8 PM	8 PM	8 PM
9 PM	9 PM	9 PM
10 PM	10 PM	10 PM
11 PM	11 PM	11 PM
12 AM	12 AM	12 AM

REMINDERS / NOTES

MEAL	MEAL	MEAL

S.L.E.E.P BEDTIME ROUTINE

ACTIVITIES FOR THE WEEK

HAPPY THOUGHTS

MONTH _____

	MONDAY	TUESDAY	WEDNESDAY	THURSDAY
4 W's WAKE ROUTINE	□ WAKE (TIME) □ WORSHIP □ WORKOUT (TIME) □ WATER (#BOTTLES)	□ WAKE (TIME) □ WORSHIP □ WORKOUT (TIME) □ WATER (#BOTTLES)	□ WAKE (TIME) □ WORSHIP □ WORKOUT (TIME) □ WATER (#BOTTLES)	□ WAKE (TIME) □ WORSHIP □ WORKOUT (TIME) □ WATER (#BOTTLES)
SELF-CARE MORNING ROUTINE	□ SHOWER / BRUSH TEETH □ DRESS / HAIR CHECK □ MAKE BED / TIDY ROOM □ BREAKFAST	□ SHOWER / BRUSH TEETH □ DRESS / HAIR CHECK □ MAKE BED / TIDY ROOM □ BREAKFAST	□ SHOWER / BRUSH TEETH □ DRESS / HAIR CHECK □ MAKE BED / TIDY ROOM □ BREAKFAST	□ SHOWER / BRUSH TEETH □ DRESS / HAIR CHECK □ MAKE BED / TIDY ROOM □ BREAKFAST
TIME	6 AM 7 AM 8 AM 9 AM 10 AM 11 AM 12 PM 1 PM 2 PM 3 PM 4 PM 5 PM 6 PM 7 PM 8 PM 9 PM 10 PM 11 PM 12 AM	6 AM 7 AM 8 AM 9 AM 10 AM 11 AM 12 PM 1 PM 2 PM 3 PM 4 PM 5 PM 6 PM 7 PM 8 PM 9 PM 10 PM 11 PM 12 AM	6 AM 7 AM 8 AM 9 AM 10 AM 11 AM 12 PM 1 PM 2 PM 3 PM 4 PM 5 PM 6 PM 7 PM 8 PM 9 PM 10P M 11 PM 12 AM	6 AM 7 AM 8 AM 9 AM 10 AM 11 AM 12 PM 1 PM 2 PM 3 PM 4 PM 5 PM 6 PM 7 PM 8 PM 9 PM 10 PM 11 PM 12 AM
	MEAL	MEAL	MEAL	MEAL

S.L.E.E.P BEDTIME ROUTINE

ACTIVITIES FOR THE WEEK

BIBLE VERSE OF THE WEEK _____

FRIDAY	SATURDAY	SUNDAY

PRAY & HUSTLE, HUSTLE & PRAY DAYTIME ROUTINE

FRIDAY	SATURDAY	SUNDAY
☐ WAKE (TIME)	☐ WAKE (TIME)	☐ WAKE (TIME)
☐ WORSHIP	☐ WORSHIP	☐ WORSHIP
☐ WORKOUT (TIME)	☐ WORKOUT (TIME)	☐ WORKOUT (TIME)
☐ WATER (#BOTTLES)	☐ WATER (#BOTTLES)	☐ WATER (#BOTTLES)
☐ SHOWER / BRUSH TEETH	☐ SHOWER / BRUSH TEETH	☐ SHOWER / BRUSH TEETH
☐ DRESS / HAIR CHECK	☐ DRESS / HAIR CHECK	☐ DRESS / HAIR CHECK
☐ MAKE BED / TIDY ROOM	☐ MAKE BED / TIDY ROOM	☐ MAKE BED / TIDY ROOM
☐ BREAKFAST	☐ BREAKFAST	☐ BREAKFAST

FRIDAY	SATURDAY	SUNDAY
6 AM	6 AM	6 AM
7 AM	7 AM	7 AM
8 AM	8 AM	8 AM
9 AM	9 AM	9 AM
10 AM	10 AM	10 AM
11 AM	11 AM	11 AM
12 PM	12 PM	12 PM
1 PM	1 PM	1 PM
2 PM	2 PM	2 PM
3 PM	3 PM	3 PM
4 PM	4 PM	4 PM
5 PM	5 PM	5 PM
6 PM	6 PM	6 PM
7 PM	7 PM	7 PM
8 PM	8 PM	8 PM
9 PM	9 PM	9 PM
10 PM	10 PM	10 PM
11 PM	11 PM	11 PM
12 AM	12 AM	12 AM

REMINDERS / NOTES

MEAL	MEAL	MEAL

S.L.E.E.P BEDTIME ROUTINE

HAPPY THOUGHTS

ACTIVITIES FOR THE WEEK

MONTH _____

	MONDAY	TUESDAY	WEDNESDAY	THURSDAY
4 W's WAKE ROUTINE	☐ WAKE (TIME) ☐ WORSHIP ☐ WORKOUT (TIME) ☐ WATER (#BOTTLES)	☐ WAKE (TIME) ☐ WORSHIP ☐ WORKOUT (TIME) ☐ WATER (#BOTTLES)	☐ WAKE (TIME) ☐ WORSHIP ☐ WORKOUT (TIME) ☐ WATER (#BOTTLES)	☐ WAKE (TIME) ☐ WORSHIP ☐ WORKOUT (TIME) ☐ WATER (#BOTTLES)
SELF-CARE MORNING ROUTINE	☐ SHOWER / BRUSH TEETH ☐ DRESS / HAIR CHECK ☐ MAKE BED / TIDY ROOM ☐ BREAKFAST	☐ SHOWER / BRUSH TEETH ☐ DRESS / HAIR CHECK ☐ MAKE BED / TIDY ROOM ☐ BREAKFAST	☐ SHOWER / BRUSH TEETH ☐ DRESS / HAIR CHECK ☐ MAKE BED / TIDY ROOM ☐ BREAKFAST	☐ SHOWER / BRUSH TEETH ☐ DRESS / HAIR CHECK ☐ MAKE BED / TIDY ROOM ☐ BREAKFAST
TIME	6 AM 7 AM 8 AM 9 AM 10 AM 11 AM 12 PM 1 PM 2 PM 3 PM 4 PM 5 PM 6 PM 7 PM 8 PM 9 PM 10 PM 11 PM 12 AM	6 AM 7 AM 8 AM 9 AM 10 AM 11 AM 12 PM 1 PM 2 PM 3 PM 4 PM 5 PM 6 PM 7 PM 8 PM 9 PM 10 PM 11 PM 12 AM	6 AM 7 AM 8 AM 9 AM 10 AM 11 AM 12 PM 1 PM 2 PM 3 PM 4 PM 5 PM 6 PM 7 PM 8 PM 9 PM 10P M 11 PM 12 AM	6 AM 7 AM 8 AM 9 AM 10 AM 11 AM 12 PM 1 PM 2 PM 3 PM 4 PM 5 PM 6 PM 7 PM 8 PM 9 PM 10 PM 11 PM 12 AM
	MEAL	MEAL	MEAL	MEAL

S.L.E.E.P BEDTIME ROUTINE

ACTIVITIES FOR THE WEEK

BIBLE VERSE OF THE WEEK _____

FRIDAY

☐ WAKE (TIME) _____
☐ WORSHIP _____
☐ WORKOUT (TIME) _____
☐ WATER (#BOTTLES) _____

☐ SHOWER / BRUSH TEETH
☐ DRESS / HAIR CHECK
☐ MAKE BED / TIDY ROOM
☐ BREAKFAST

6 AM _____
7 AM _____
8 AM _____
9 AM _____
10 AM _____
11 AM _____
12 PM _____
1 PM _____
2 PM _____
3 PM _____
4 PM _____
5 PM _____
6 PM _____
7 PM _____
8 PM _____
9 PM _____
10 PM _____
11 PM _____
12 AM _____

MEAL

SATURDAY

☐ WAKE (TIME) _____
☐ WORSHIP _____
☐ WORKOUT (TIME) _____
☐ WATER (#BOTTLES) _____

☐ SHOWER / BRUSH TEETH
☐ DRESS / HAIR CHECK
☐ MAKE BED / TIDY ROOM
☐ BREAKFAST

6 AM _____
7 AM _____
8 AM _____
9 AM _____
10 AM _____
11 AM _____
12 PM _____
1 PM _____
2 PM _____
3 PM _____
4 PM _____
5 PM _____
6 PM _____
7 PM _____
8 PM _____
9 PM _____
10 PM _____
11 PM _____
12 AM _____

MEAL

SUNDAY

☐ WAKE (TIME) _____
☐ WORSHIP _____
☐ WORKOUT (TIME) _____
☐ WATER (#BOTTLES) _____

☐ SHOWER / BRUSH TEETH
☐ DRESS / HAIR CHECK
☐ MAKE BED / TIDY ROOM
☐ BREAKFAST

6 AM _____
7 AM _____
8 AM _____
9 AM _____
10 AM _____
11 AM _____
12 PM _____
1 PM _____
2 PM _____
3 PM _____
4 PM _____
5 PM _____
6 PM _____
7 PM _____
8 PM _____
9 PM _____
10 PM _____
11 PM _____
12 AM _____

MEAL

PRAY & HUSTLE, HUSTLE & PRAY DAYTIME ROUTINE

REMINDERS / NOTES

HAPPY THOUGHTS

S.L.E.E.P BEDTIME ROUTINE

ACTIVITIES FOR THE WEEK

MONTH			

	MONDAY	TUESDAY	WEDNESDAY	THURSDAY
4 W's WAKE ROUTINE	☐ WAKE (TIME)	☐ WAKE (TIME)	☐ WAKE (TIME)	☐ WAKE (TIME)
	☐ WORSHIP	☐ WORSHIP	☐ WORSHIP	☐ WORSHIP
	☐ WORKOUT (TIME)	☐ WORKOUT (TIME)	☐ WORKOUT (TIME)	☐ WORKOUT (TIME)
	☐ WATER (#BOTTLES)	☐ WATER (#BOTTLES)	☐ WATER (#BOTTLES)	☐ WATER (#BOTTLES)
SELF-CARE MORNING ROUTINE	☐ SHOWER / BRUSH TEETH	☐ SHOWER / BRUSH TEETH	☐ SHOWER / BRUSH TEETH	☐ SHOWER / BRUSH TEETH
	☐ DRESS / HAIR CHECK	☐ DRESS / HAIR CHECK	☐ DRESS / HAIR CHECK	☐ DRESS / HAIR CHECK
	☐ MAKE BED / TIDY ROOM	☐ MAKE BED / TIDY ROOM	☐ MAKE BED / TIDY ROOM	☐ MAKE BED / TIDY ROOM
	☐ BREAKFAST	☐ BREAKFAST	☐ BREAKFAST	☐ BREAKFAST
TIME	6 AM	6 AM	6 AM	6 AM
	7 AM	7 AM	7 AM	7 AM
	8 AM	8 AM	8 AM	8 AM
	9 AM	9 AM	9 AM	9 AM
	10 AM	10 AM	10 AM	10 AM
	11 AM	11 AM	11 AM	11 AM
	12 PM	12 PM	12 PM	12 PM
	1 PM	1 PM	1 PM	1 PM
	2 PM	2 PM	2 PM	2 PM
	3 PM	3 PM	3 PM	3 PM
	4 PM	4 PM	4 PM	4 PM
	5 PM	5 PM	5 PM	5 PM
	6 PM	6 PM	6 PM	6 PM
	7 PM	7 PM	7 PM	7 PM
	8 PM	8 PM	8 PM	8 PM
	9 PM	9 PM	9 PM	9 PM
	10 PM	10 PM	10P M	10 PM
	11 PM	11 PM	11 PM	11 PM
	12 AM	12 AM	12 AM	12 AM
	MEAL	MEAL	MEAL	MEAL

S.L.E.E.P BEDTIME ROUTINE

ACTIVITIES FOR THE WEEK

BIBLE VERSE OF THE WEEK _____

FRIDAY	SATURDAY	SUNDAY
□ WAKE (TIME)	□ WAKE (TIME)	□ WAKE (TIME)
□ WORSHIP	□ WORSHIP	□ WORSHIP
□ WORKOUT (TIME)	□ WORKOUT (TIME)	□ WORKOUT (TIME)
□ WATER (#BOTTLES)	□ WATER (#BOTTLES)	□ WATER (#BOTTLES)

PRAY & HUSTLE, HUSTLE & PRAY DAYTIME ROUTINE

FRIDAY	SATURDAY	SUNDAY
□ SHOWER / BRUSH TEETH	□ SHOWER / BRUSH TEETH	□ SHOWER / BRUSH TEETH
□ DRESS / HAIR CHECK	□ DRESS / HAIR CHECK	□ DRESS / HAIR CHECK
□ MAKE BED / TIDY ROOM	□ MAKE BED / TIDY ROOM	□ MAKE BED / TIDY ROOM
□ BREAKFAST	□ BREAKFAST	□ BREAKFAST

FRIDAY	SATURDAY	SUNDAY
6 AM	6 AM	6 AM
7 AM	7 AM	7 AM
8 AM	8 AM	8 AM
9 AM	9 AM	9 AM
10 AM	10 AM	10 AM
11 AM	11 AM	11 AM
12 PM	12 PM	12 PM
1 PM	1 PM	1 PM
2 PM	2 PM	2 PM
3 PM	3 PM	3 PM
4 PM	4 PM	4 PM
5 PM	5 PM	5 PM
6 PM	6 PM	6 PM
7 PM	7 PM	7 PM
8 PM	8 PM	8 PM
9 PM	9 PM	9 PM
10 PM	10 PM	10 PM
11 PM	11 PM	11 PM
12 AM	12 AM	12 AM

REMINDERS / NOTES

MEAL	MEAL	MEAL

S.L.E.E.P BEDTIME ROUTINE

HAPPY THOUGHTS

ACTIVITIES FOR THE WEEK

	MONDAY	TUESDAY	WEDNESDAY	THURSDAY
4 W's WAKE ROUTINE	☐ WAKE (TIME) ☐ WORSHIP ☐ WORKOUT (TIME) ☐ WATER (#BOTTLES)	☐ WAKE (TIME) ☐ WORSHIP ☐ WORKOUT (TIME) ☐ WATER (#BOTTLES)	☐ WAKE (TIME) ☐ WORSHIP ☐ WORKOUT (TIME) ☐ WATER (#BOTTLES)	☐ WAKE (TIME) ☐ WORSHIP ☐ WORKOUT (TIME) ☐ WATER (#BOTTLES)
SELF-CARE MORNING ROUTINE	☐ SHOWER / BRUSH TEETH ☐ DRESS / HAIR CHECK ☐ MAKE BED / TIDY ROOM ☐ BREAKFAST	☐ SHOWER / BRUSH TEETH ☐ DRESS / HAIR CHECK ☐ MAKE BED / TIDY ROOM ☐ BREAKFAST	☐ SHOWER / BRUSH TEETH ☐ DRESS / HAIR CHECK ☐ MAKE BED / TIDY ROOM ☐ BREAKFAST	☐ SHOWER / BRUSH TEETH ☐ DRESS / HAIR CHECK ☐ MAKE BED / TIDY ROOM ☐ BREAKFAST
TIME	6 AM 7 AM 8 AM 9 AM 10 AM 11 AM 12 PM 1 PM 2 PM 3 PM 4 PM 5 PM 6 PM 7 PM 8 PM 9 PM 10 PM 11 PM 12 AM	6 AM 7 AM 8 AM 9 AM 10 AM 11 AM 12 PM 1 PM 2 PM 3 PM 4 PM 5 PM 6 PM 7 PM 8 PM 9 PM 10 PM 11 PM 12 AM	6 AM 7 AM 8 AM 9 AM 10 AM 11 AM 12 PM 1 PM 2 PM 3 PM 4 PM 5 PM 6 PM 7 PM 8 PM 9 PM 10P M 11 PM 12 AM	6 AM 7 AM 8 AM 9 AM 10 AM 11 AM 12 PM 1 PM 2 PM 3 PM 4 PM 5 PM 6 PM 7 PM 8 PM 9 PM 10 PM 11 PM 12 AM
	MEAL	MEAL	MEAL	MEAL
	_____	_____	_____	_____

S.L.E.E.P BEDTIME ROUTINE

_____ _____ _____ _____

ACTIVITIES FOR THE WEEK

_____ _____ _____ _____

BIBLE VERSE OF THE WEEK _____

FRIDAY	SATURDAY	SUNDAY	
			PRAY & HUSTLE, HUSTLE & PRAY **DAYTIME ROUTINE**
☐ WAKE (TIME)	☐ WAKE (TIME)	☐ WAKE (TIME)	
☐ WORSHIP	☐ WORSHIP	☐ WORSHIP	
☐ WORKOUT (TIME)	☐ WORKOUT (TIME)	☐ WORKOUT (TIME)	
☐ WATER (#BOTTLES)	☐ WATER (#BOTTLES)	☐ WATER (#BOTTLES)	_____
☐ SHOWER / BRUSH TEETH	☐ SHOWER / BRUSH TEETH	☐ SHOWER / BRUSH TEETH	_____
☐ DRESS / HAIR CHECK	☐ DRESS / HAIR CHECK	☐ DRESS / HAIR CHECK	
☐ MAKE BED / TIDY ROOM	☐ MAKE BED / TIDY ROOM	☐ MAKE BED / TIDY ROOM	_____
☐ BREAKFAST	☐ BREAKFAST	☐ BREAKFAST	
			_____
6 AM	6 AM	6 AM	
7 AM	7 AM	7 AM	
8 AM	8 AM	8 AM	
9 AM	9 AM	9 AM	**REMINDERS / NOTES**
10 AM	10 AM	10 AM	
11 AM	11 AM	11 AM	
12 PM	12 PM	12 PM	_____
1 PM	1 PM	1 PM	
2 PM	2 PM	2 PM	_____
3 PM	3 PM	3 PM	
4 PM	4 PM	4 PM	_____
5 PM	5 PM	5 PM	
6 PM	6 PM	6 PM	_____
7 PM	7 PM	7 PM	
8 PM	8 PM	8 PM	_____
9 PM	9 PM	9 PM	
10 PM	10 PM	10 PM	
11 PM	11 PM	11 PM	
12 AM	12 AM	12 AM	

MEAL	MEAL	MEAL

HAPPY THOUGHTS

S.L.E.E.P BEDTIME ROUTINE

ACTIVITIES FOR THE WEEK

MONTH _____

	MONDAY	TUESDAY	WEDNESDAY	THURSDAY
4 W's WAKE ROUTINE	□ WAKE (TIME)	□ WAKE (TIME)	□ WAKE (TIME)	□ WAKE (TIME)
	□ WORSHIP	□ WORSHIP	□ WORSHIP	□ WORSHIP
	□ WORKOUT (TIME)	□ WORKOUT (TIME)	□ WORKOUT (TIME)	□ WORKOUT (TIME)
	□ WATER (#BOTTLES)	□ WATER (#BOTTLES)	□ WATER (#BOTTLES)	□ WATER (#BOTTLES)
SELF-CARE MORNING ROUTINE	□ SHOWER / BRUSH TEETH	□ SHOWER / BRUSH TEETH	□ SHOWER / BRUSH TEETH	□ SHOWER / BRUSH TEETH
	□ DRESS / HAIR CHECK	□ DRESS / HAIR CHECK	□ DRESS / HAIR CHECK	□ DRESS / HAIR CHECK
	□ MAKE BED / TIDY ROOM	□ MAKE BED / TIDY ROOM	□ MAKE BED / TIDY ROOM	□ MAKE BED / TIDY ROOM
	□ BREAKFAST	□ BREAKFAST	□ BREAKFAST	□ BREAKFAST
TIME	6 AM	6 AM	6 AM	6 AM
	7 AM	7 AM	7 AM	7 AM
	8 AM	8 AM	8 AM	8 AM
	9 AM	9 AM	9 AM	9 AM
	10 AM	10 AM	10 AM	10 AM
	11 AM	11 AM	11 AM	11 AM
	12 PM	12 PM	12 PM	12 PM
	1 PM	1 PM	1 PM	1 PM
	2 PM	2 PM	2 PM	2 PM
	3 PM	3 PM	3 PM	3 PM
	4 PM	4 PM	4 PM	4 PM
	5 PM	5 PM	5 PM	5 PM
	6 PM	6 PM	6 PM	6 PM
	7 PM	7 PM	7 PM	7 PM
	8 PM	8 PM	8 PM	8 PM
	9 PM	9 PM	9 PM	9 PM
	10 PM	10 PM	10P M	10 PM
	11 PM	11 PM	11 PM	11 PM
	12 AM	12 AM	12 AM	12 AM
	MEAL	MEAL	MEAL	MEAL

S.L.E.E.P BEDTIME ROUTINE

ACTIVITIES FOR THE WEEK

BIBLE VERSE OF THE WEEK _____

FRIDAY	SATURDAY	SUNDAY
			PRAY & HUSTLE, HUSTLE & PRAY

FRIDAY

☐ WAKE (TIME) _____
☐ WORSHIP
☐ WORKOUT (TIME) _____
☐ WATER (#BOTTLES)

☐ SHOWER / BRUSH TEETH
☐ DRESS / HAIR CHECK
☐ MAKE BED / TIDY ROOM
☐ BREAKFAST

SATURDAY

☐ WAKE (TIME) _____
☐ WORSHIP
☐ WORKOUT (TIME) _____
☐ WATER (#BOTTLES)

☐ SHOWER / BRUSH TEETH
☐ DRESS / HAIR CHECK
☐ MAKE BED / TIDY ROOM
☐ BREAKFAST

SUNDAY

☐ WAKE (TIME) _____
☐ WORSHIP
☐ WORKOUT (TIME) _____
☐ WATER (#BOTTLES)

☐ SHOWER / BRUSH TEETH
☐ DRESS / HAIR CHECK
☐ MAKE BED / TIDY ROOM
☐ BREAKFAST

PRAY & HUSTLE, HUSTLE & PRAY DAYTIME ROUTINE

FRIDAY	SATURDAY	SUNDAY
6 AM	6 AM	6 AM
7 AM	7 AM	7 AM
8 AM	8 AM	8 AM
9 AM	9 AM	9 AM
10 AM	10 AM	10 AM
11 AM	11 AM	11 AM
12 PM	12 PM	12 PM
1 PM	1 PM	1 PM
2 PM	2 PM	2 PM
3 PM	3 PM	3 PM
4 PM	4 PM	4 PM
5 PM	5 PM	5 PM
6 PM	6 PM	6 PM
7 PM	7 PM	7 PM
8 PM	8 PM	8 PM
9 PM	9 PM	9 PM
10 PM	10 PM	10 PM
11 PM	11 PM	11 PM
12 AM	12 AM	12 AM

REMINDERS / NOTES

MEAL   MEAL   MEAL

S.L.E.E.P BEDTIME ROUTINE

HAPPY THOUGHTS
_____
_____
_____
_____
_____

ACTIVITIES FOR THE WEEK

	MONDAY	TUESDAY	WEDNESDAY	THURSDAY
4 W's WAKE ROUTINE	□ WAKE (TIME) □ WORSHIP □ WORKOUT (TIME) □ WATER (#BOTTLES)	□ WAKE (TIME) □ WORSHIP □ WORKOUT (TIME) □ WATER (#BOTTLES)	□ WAKE (TIME) □ WORSHIP □ WORKOUT (TIME) □ WATER (#BOTTLES)	□ WAKE (TIME) □ WORSHIP □ WORKOUT (TIME) □ WATER (#BOTTLES)
SELF-CARE MORNING ROUTINE	□ SHOWER / BRUSH TEETH □ DRESS / HAIR CHECK □ MAKE BED / TIDY ROOM □ BREAKFAST	□ SHOWER / BRUSH TEETH □ DRESS / HAIR CHECK □ MAKE BED / TIDY ROOM □ BREAKFAST	□ SHOWER / BRUSH TEETH □ DRESS / HAIR CHECK □ MAKE BED / TIDY ROOM □ BREAKFAST	□ SHOWER / BRUSH TEETH □ DRESS / HAIR CHECK □ MAKE BED / TIDY ROOM □ BREAKFAST
TIME	6 AM 7 AM 8 AM 9 AM 10 AM 11 AM 12 PM 1 PM 2 PM 3 PM 4 PM 5 PM 6 PM 7 PM 8 PM 9 PM 10 PM 11 PM 12 AM	6 AM 7 AM 8 AM 9 AM 10 AM 11 AM 12 PM 1 PM 2 PM 3 PM 4 PM 5 PM 6 PM 7 PM 8 PM 9 PM 10 PM 11 PM 12 AM	6 AM 7 AM 8 AM 9 AM 10 AM 11 AM 12 PM 1 PM 2 PM 3 PM 4 PM 5 PM 6 PM 7 PM 8 PM 9 PM 10P M 11 PM 12 AM	6 AM 7 AM 8 AM 9 AM 10 AM 11 AM 12 PM 1 PM 2 PM 3 PM 4 PM 5 PM 6 PM 7 PM 8 PM 9 PM 10 PM 11 PM 12 AM
	MEAL	**MEAL**	**MEAL**	**MEAL**

MONTH _____

S.L.E.E.P BEDTIME ROUTINE

ACTIVITIES FOR THE WEEK

BIBLE VERSE OF THE WEEK _____

FRIDAY

- ☐ WAKE (TIME) _____
- ☐ WORSHIP _____
- ☐ WORKOUT (TIME) _____
- ☐ WATER (#BOTTLES) _____

- ☐ SHOWER / BRUSH TEETH
- ☐ DRESS / HAIR CHECK
- ☐ MAKE BED / TIDY ROOM
- ☐ BREAKFAST

6 AM _____
7 AM _____
8 AM _____
9 AM _____
10 AM _____
11 AM _____
12 PM _____
1 PM _____
2 PM _____
3 PM _____
4 PM _____
5 PM _____
6 PM _____
7 PM _____
8 PM _____
9 PM _____
10 PM _____
11 PM _____
12 AM _____

SATURDAY

- ☐ WAKE (TIME) _____
- ☐ WORSHIP _____
- ☐ WORKOUT (TIME) _____
- ☐ WATER (#BOTTLES) _____

- ☐ SHOWER / BRUSH TEETH
- ☐ DRESS / HAIR CHECK
- ☐ MAKE BED / TIDY ROOM
- ☐ BREAKFAST

6 AM _____
7 AM _____
8 AM _____
9 AM _____
10 AM _____
11 AM _____
12 PM _____
1 PM _____
2 PM _____
3 PM _____
4 PM _____
5 PM _____
6 PM _____
7 PM _____
8 PM _____
9 PM _____
10 PM _____
11 PM _____
12 AM _____

SUNDAY

- ☐ WAKE (TIME) _____
- ☐ WORSHIP _____
- ☐ WORKOUT (TIME) _____
- ☐ WATER (#BOTTLES) _____

- ☐ SHOWER / BRUSH TEETH
- ☐ DRESS / HAIR CHECK
- ☐ MAKE BED / TIDY ROOM
- ☐ BREAKFAST

6 AM _____
7 AM _____
8 AM _____
9 AM _____
10 AM _____
11 AM _____
12 PM _____
1 PM _____
2 PM _____
3 PM _____
4 PM _____
5 PM _____
6 PM _____
7 PM _____
8 PM _____
9 PM _____
10 PM _____
11 PM _____
12 AM _____

PRAY & HUSTLE, HUSTLE & PRAY DAYTIME ROUTINE

_____
_____
_____
_____
_____

REMINDERS / NOTES

_____
_____
_____
_____
_____
_____

HAPPY THOUGHTS

_____
_____
_____
_____
_____

MEAL   MEAL   MEAL
_____   _____   _____
_____   _____   _____

S.L.E.E.P BEDTIME ROUTINE

_____   _____   _____
_____   _____   _____

ACTIVITIES FOR THE WEEK

_____   _____   _____

MONTH _____

	MONDAY	TUESDAY	WEDNESDAY	THURSDAY
4 W's WAKE ROUTINE	□ WAKE (TIME)	□ WAKE (TIME)	□ WAKE (TIME)	□ WAKE (TIME)
	□ WORSHIP	□ WORSHIP	□ WORSHIP	□ WORSHIP
	□ WORKOUT (TIME)	□ WORKOUT (TIME)	□ WORKOUT (TIME)	□ WORKOUT (TIME)
	□ WATER (#BOTTLES)	□ WATER (#BOTTLES)	□ WATER (#BOTTLES)	□ WATER (#BOTTLES)
SELF-CARE MORNING ROUTINE	□ SHOWER / BRUSH TEETH	□ SHOWER / BRUSH TEETH	□ SHOWER / BRUSH TEETH	□ SHOWER / BRUSH TEETH
	□ DRESS / HAIR CHECK	□ DRESS / HAIR CHECK	□ DRESS / HAIR CHECK	□ DRESS / HAIR CHECK
	□ MAKE BED / TIDY ROOM	□ MAKE BED / TIDY ROOM	□ MAKE BED / TIDY ROOM	□ MAKE BED / TIDY ROOM
	□ BREAKFAST	□ BREAKFAST	□ BREAKFAST	□ BREAKFAST
TIME	6 AM	6 AM	6 AM	6 AM
	7 AM	7 AM	7 AM	7 AM
	8 AM	8 AM	8 AM	8 AM
	9 AM	9 AM	9 AM	9 AM
	10 AM	10 AM	10 AM	10 AM
	11 AM	11 AM	11 AM	11 AM
	12 PM	12 PM	12 PM	12 PM
	1 PM	1 PM	1 PM	1 PM
	2 PM	2 PM	2 PM	2 PM
	3 PM	3 PM	3 PM	3 PM
	4 PM	4 PM	4 PM	4 PM
	5 PM	5 PM	5 PM	5 PM
	6 PM	6 PM	6 PM	6 PM
	7 PM	7 PM	7 PM	7 PM
	8 PM	8 PM	8 PM	8 PM
	9 PM	9 PM	9 PM	9 PM
	10 PM	10 PM	10P M	10 PM
	11 PM	11 PM	11 PM	11 PM
	12 AM	12 AM	12 AM	12 AM
	MEAL	**MEAL**	**MEAL**	**MEAL**

S.L.E.E.P BEDTIME ROUTINE

ACTIVITIES FOR THE WEEK

BIBLE VERSE OF THE WEEK _____

FRIDAY	SATURDAY	SUNDAY
□ WAKE (TIME)	□ WAKE (TIME)	□ WAKE (TIME)
□ WORSHIP	□ WORSHIP	□ WORSHIP
□ WORKOUT (TIME)	□ WORKOUT (TIME)	□ WORKOUT (TIME)
□ WATER (#BOTTLES)	□ WATER (#BOTTLES)	□ WATER (#BOTTLES)
□ SHOWER / BRUSH TEETH	□ SHOWER / BRUSH TEETH	□ SHOWER / BRUSH TEETH
□ DRESS / HAIR CHECK	□ DRESS / HAIR CHECK	□ DRESS / HAIR CHECK
□ MAKE BED / TIDY ROOM	□ MAKE BED / TIDY ROOM	□ MAKE BED / TIDY ROOM
□ BREAKFAST	□ BREAKFAST	□ BREAKFAST

PRAY & HUSTLE, HUSTLE & PRAY DAYTIME ROUTINE

FRIDAY	SATURDAY	SUNDAY
6 AM	6 AM	6 AM
7 AM	7 AM	7 AM
8 AM	8 AM	8 AM
9 AM	9 AM	9 AM
10 AM	10 AM	10 AM
11 AM	11 AM	11 AM
12 PM	12 PM	12 PM
1 PM	1 PM	1 PM
2 PM	2 PM	2 PM
3 PM	3 PM	3 PM
4 PM	4 PM	4 PM
5 PM	5 PM	5 PM
6 PM	6 PM	6 PM
7 PM	7 PM	7 PM
8 PM	8 PM	8 PM
9 PM	9 PM	9 PM
10 PM	10 PM	10 PM
11 PM	11 PM	11 PM
12 AM	12 AM	12 AM

REMINDERS / NOTES

MEAL   MEAL   MEAL

S.L.E.E.P BEDTIME ROUTINE

ACTIVITIES FOR THE WEEK

HAPPY THOUGHTS

MONTH _____

	MONDAY	TUESDAY	WEDNESDAY	THURSDAY
4 W's WAKE ROUTINE	□ WAKE (TIME) □ WORSHIP □ WORKOUT (TIME) □ WATER (#BOTTLES)	□ WAKE (TIME) □ WORSHIP □ WORKOUT (TIME) □ WATER (#BOTTLES)	□ WAKE (TIME) □ WORSHIP □ WORKOUT (TIME) □ WATER (#BOTTLES)	□ WAKE (TIME) □ WORSHIP □ WORKOUT (TIME) □ WATER (#BOTTLES)
SELF-CARE MORNING ROUTINE	□ SHOWER / BRUSH TEETH □ DRESS / HAIR CHECK □ MAKE BED / TIDY ROOM □ BREAKFAST	□ SHOWER / BRUSH TEETH □ DRESS / HAIR CHECK □ MAKE BED / TIDY ROOM □ BREAKFAST	□ SHOWER / BRUSH TEETH □ DRESS / HAIR CHECK □ MAKE BED / TIDY ROOM □ BREAKFAST	□ SHOWER / BRUSH TEETH □ DRESS / HAIR CHECK □ MAKE BED / TIDY ROOM □ BREAKFAST
TIME	6 AM 7 AM 8 AM 9 AM 10 AM 11 AM 12 PM 1 PM 2 PM 3 PM 4 PM 5 PM 6 PM 7 PM 8 PM 9 PM 10 PM 11 PM 12 AM	6 AM 7 AM 8 AM 9 AM 10 AM 11 AM 12 PM 1 PM 2 PM 3 PM 4 PM 5 PM 6 PM 7 PM 8 PM 9 PM 10 PM 11 PM 12 AM	6 AM 7 AM 8 AM 9 AM 10 AM 11 AM 12 PM 1 PM 2 PM 3 PM 4 PM 5 PM 6 PM 7 PM 8 PM 9 PM 10P M 11 PM 12 AM	6 AM 7 AM 8 AM 9 AM 10 AM 11 AM 12 PM 1 PM 2 PM 3 PM 4 PM 5 PM 6 PM 7 PM 8 PM 9 PM 10 PM 11 PM 12 AM
	MEAL _____	**MEAL** _____	**MEAL** _____	**MEAL** _____

S.L.E.E.P BEDTIME ROUTINE

_____ _____ _____ _____

_____ _____ _____ _____

ACTIVITIES FOR THE WEEK

_____ _____ _____ _____

BIBLE VERSE OF THE WEEK _____

FRIDAY	SATURDAY	SUNDAY
□ WAKE (TIME)	□ WAKE (TIME)	□ WAKE (TIME)
□ WORSHIP	□ WORSHIP	□ WORSHIP
□ WORKOUT (TIME)	□ WORKOUT (TIME)	□ WORKOUT (TIME)
□ WATER (#BOTTLES)	□ WATER (#BOTTLES)	□ WATER (#BOTTLES)

PRAY & HUSTLE, HUSTLE & PRAY DAYTIME ROUTINE

_____
_____
_____
_____

FRIDAY	SATURDAY	SUNDAY
□ SHOWER / BRUSH TEETH	□ SHOWER / BRUSH TEETH	□ SHOWER / BRUSH TEETH
□ DRESS / HAIR CHECK	□ DRESS / HAIR CHECK	□ DRESS / HAIR CHECK
□ MAKE BED / TIDY ROOM	□ MAKE BED / TIDY ROOM	□ MAKE BED / TIDY ROOM
□ BREAKFAST	□ BREAKFAST	□ BREAKFAST

FRIDAY	SATURDAY	SUNDAY
6 AM	6 AM	6 AM
7 AM	7 AM	7 AM
8 AM	8 AM	8 AM
9 AM	9 AM	9 AM
10 AM	10 AM	10 AM
11 AM	11 AM	11 AM
12 PM	12 PM	12 PM
1 PM	1 PM	1 PM
2 PM	2 PM	2 PM
3 PM	3 PM	3 PM
4 PM	4 PM	4 PM
5 PM	5 PM	5 PM
6 PM	6 PM	6 PM
7 PM	7 PM	7 PM
8 PM	8 PM	8 PM
9 PM	9 PM	9 PM
10 PM	10 PM	10 PM
11 PM	11 PM	11 PM
12 AM	12 AM	12 AM

REMINDERS / NOTES

_____
_____
_____
_____
_____
_____

MEAL	MEAL	MEAL

HAPPY THOUGHTS

_____
_____
_____
_____
_____

S.L.E.E.P BEDTIME ROUTINE

ACTIVITIES FOR THE WEEK

MONTH			

	MONDAY	TUESDAY	WEDNESDAY	THURSDAY
4 W's WAKE ROUTINE	□ WAKE (TIME) □ WORSHIP □ WORKOUT (TIME) □ WATER (#BOTTLES)	□ WAKE (TIME) □ WORSHIP □ WORKOUT (TIME) □ WATER (#BOTTLES)	□ WAKE (TIME) □ WORSHIP □ WORKOUT (TIME) □ WATER (#BOTTLES)	□ WAKE (TIME) □ WORSHIP □ WORKOUT (TIME) □ WATER (#BOTTLES)
SELF-CARE MORNING ROUTINE	□ SHOWER / BRUSH TEETH □ DRESS / HAIR CHECK □ MAKE BED / TIDY ROOM □ BREAKFAST	□ SHOWER / BRUSH TEETH □ DRESS / HAIR CHECK □ MAKE BED / TIDY ROOM □ BREAKFAST	□ SHOWER / BRUSH TEETH □ DRESS / HAIR CHECK □ MAKE BED / TIDY ROOM □ BREAKFAST	□ SHOWER / BRUSH TEETH □ DRESS / HAIR CHECK □ MAKE BED / TIDY ROOM □ BREAKFAST
TIME	6 AM 7 AM 8 AM 9 AM 10 AM 11 AM 12 PM 1 PM 2 PM 3 PM 4 PM 5 PM 6 PM 7 PM 8 PM 9 PM 10 PM 11 PM 12 AM	6 AM 7 AM 8 AM 9 AM 10 AM 11 AM 12 PM 1 PM 2 PM 3 PM 4 PM 5 PM 6 PM 7 PM 8 PM 9 PM 10 PM 11 PM 12 AM	6 AM 7 AM 8 AM 9 AM 10 AM 11 AM 12 PM 1 PM 2 PM 3 PM 4 PM 5 PM 6 PM 7 PM 8 PM 9 PM 10P M 11 PM 12 AM	6 AM 7 AM 8 AM 9 AM 10 AM 11 AM 12 PM 1 PM 2 PM 3 PM 4 PM 5 PM 6 PM 7 PM 8 PM 9 PM 10 PM 11 PM 12 AM
	MEAL	MEAL	MEAL	MEAL

S.L.E.E.P BEDTIME ROUTINE

ACTIVITIES FOR THE WEEK

BIBLE VERSE OF THE WEEK _____

FRIDAY	SATURDAY	SUNDAY	
			PRAY & HUSTLE, HUSTLE & PRAY DAYTIME ROUTINE
☐ WAKE (TIME)	☐ WAKE (TIME)	☐ WAKE (TIME)	
☐ WORSHIP	☐ WORSHIP	☐ WORSHIP	
☐ WORKOUT (TIME)	☐ WORKOUT (TIME)	☐ WORKOUT (TIME)	
☐ WATER (#BOTTLES)	☐ WATER (#BOTTLES)	☐ WATER (#BOTTLES)	
☐ SHOWER / BRUSH TEETH	☐ SHOWER / BRUSH TEETH	☐ SHOWER / BRUSH TEETH	
☐ DRESS / HAIR CHECK	☐ DRESS / HAIR CHECK	☐ DRESS / HAIR CHECK	
☐ MAKE BED / TIDY ROOM	☐ MAKE BED / TIDY ROOM	☐ MAKE BED / TIDY ROOM	
☐ BREAKFAST	☐ BREAKFAST	☐ BREAKFAST	

FRIDAY	SATURDAY	SUNDAY	
6 AM	6 AM	6 AM	
7 AM	7 AM	7 AM	
8 AM	8 AM	8 AM	
9 AM	9 AM	9 AM	**REMINDERS / NOTES**
10 AM	10 AM	10 AM	
11 AM	11 AM	11 AM	
12 PM	12 PM	12 PM	
1 PM	1 PM	1 PM	
2 PM	2 PM	2 PM	
3 PM	3 PM	3 PM	
4 PM	4 PM	4 PM	
5 PM	5 PM	5 PM	
6 PM	6 PM	6 PM	
7 PM	7 PM	7 PM	
8 PM	8 PM	8 PM	
9 PM	9 PM	9 PM	
10 PM	10 PM	10 PM	
11 PM	11 PM	11 PM	
12 AM	12 AM	12 AM	

MEAL	MEAL	MEAL

S.L.E.E.P BEDTIME ROUTINE

HAPPY THOUGHTS

ACTIVITIES FOR THE WEEK

	MONDAY	TUESDAY	WEDNESDAY	THURSDAY
4 W's WAKE ROUTINE	☐ WAKE (TIME)	☐ WAKE (TIME)	☐ WAKE (TIME)	☐ WAKE (TIME)
	☐ WORSHIP	☐ WORSHIP	☐ WORSHIP	☐ WORSHIP
	☐ WORKOUT (TIME)	☐ WORKOUT (TIME)	☐ WORKOUT (TIME)	☐ WORKOUT (TIME)
	☐ WATER (#BOTTLES)	☐ WATER (#BOTTLES)	☐ WATER (#BOTTLES)	☐ WATER (#BOTTLES)
SELF-CARE MORNING ROUTINE	☐ SHOWER / BRUSH TEETH	☐ SHOWER / BRUSH TEETH	☐ SHOWER / BRUSH TEETH	☐ SHOWER / BRUSH TEETH
	☐ DRESS / HAIR CHECK	☐ DRESS / HAIR CHECK	☐ DRESS / HAIR CHECK	☐ DRESS / HAIR CHECK
	☐ MAKE BED / TIDY ROOM	☐ MAKE BED / TIDY ROOM	☐ MAKE BED / TIDY ROOM	☐ MAKE BED / TIDY ROOM
	☐ BREAKFAST	☐ BREAKFAST	☐ BREAKFAST	☐ BREAKFAST
TIME	6 AM	6 AM	6 AM	6 AM
	7 AM	7 AM	7 AM	7 AM
	8 AM	8 AM	8 AM	8 AM
	9 AM	9 AM	9 AM	9 AM
	10 AM	10 AM	10 AM	10 AM
	11 AM	11 AM	11 AM	11 AM
	12 PM	12 PM	12 PM	12 PM
	1 PM	1 PM	1 PM	1 PM
	2 PM	2 PM	2 PM	2 PM
	3 PM	3 PM	3 PM	3 PM
	4 PM	4 PM	4 PM	4 PM
	5 PM	5 PM	5 PM	5 PM
	6 PM	6 PM	6 PM	6 PM
	7 PM	7 PM	7 PM	7 PM
	8 PM	8 PM	8 PM	8 PM
	9 PM	9 PM	9 PM	9 PM
	10 PM	10 PM	10P M	10 PM
	11 PM	11 PM	11 PM	11 PM
	12 AM	12 AM	12 AM	12 AM
	MEAL	**MEAL**	**MEAL**	**MEAL**

S.L.E.E.P BEDTIME ROUTINE

ACTIVITIES FOR THE WEEK

BIBLE VERSE OF THE WEEK _____

FRIDAY

- ☐ WAKE (TIME) _____
- ☐ WORSHIP _____
- ☐ WORKOUT (TIME) _____
- ☐ WATER (#BOTTLES) _____

- ☐ SHOWER / BRUSH TEETH
- ☐ DRESS / HAIR CHECK
- ☐ MAKE BED / TIDY ROOM
- ☐ BREAKFAST

SATURDAY

- ☐ WAKE (TIME) _____
- ☐ WORSHIP _____
- ☐ WORKOUT (TIME) _____
- ☐ WATER (#BOTTLES) _____

- ☐ SHOWER / BRUSH TEETH
- ☐ DRESS / HAIR CHECK
- ☐ MAKE BED / TIDY ROOM
- ☐ BREAKFAST

SUNDAY

- ☐ WAKE (TIME) _____
- ☐ WORSHIP _____
- ☐ WORKOUT (TIME) _____
- ☐ WATER (#BOTTLES) _____

- ☐ SHOWER / BRUSH TEETH
- ☐ DRESS / HAIR CHECK
- ☐ MAKE BED / TIDY ROOM
- ☐ BREAKFAST

PRAY & HUSTLE, HUSTLE & PRAY DAYTIME ROUTINE

FRIDAY	SATURDAY	SUNDAY
6 AM	6 AM	6 AM
7 AM	7 AM	7 AM
8 AM	8 AM	8 AM
9 AM	9 AM	9 AM
10 AM	10 AM	10 AM
11 AM	11 AM	11 AM
12 PM	12 PM	12 PM
1 PM	1 PM	1 PM
2 PM	2 PM	2 PM
3 PM	3 PM	3 PM
4 PM	4 PM	4 PM
5 PM	5 PM	5 PM
6 PM	6 PM	6 PM
7 PM	7 PM	7 PM
8 PM	8 PM	8 PM
9 PM	9 PM	9 PM
10 PM	10 PM	10 PM
11 PM	11 PM	11 PM
12 AM	12 AM	12 AM

REMINDERS / NOTES

MEAL _____   MEAL _____   MEAL _____

S.L.E.E.P BEDTIME ROUTINE

HAPPY THOUGHTS

ACTIVITIES FOR THE WEEK

MONTH _____

	MONDAY	TUESDAY	WEDNESDAY	THURSDAY
4 W's WAKE ROUTINE	□ WAKE (TIME) □ WORSHIP □ WORKOUT (TIME) □ WATER (#BOTTLES)	□ WAKE (TIME) □ WORSHIP □ WORKOUT (TIME) □ WATER (#BOTTLES)	□ WAKE (TIME) □ WORSHIP □ WORKOUT (TIME) □ WATER (#BOTTLES)	□ WAKE (TIME) □ WORSHIP □ WORKOUT (TIME) □ WATER (#BOTTLES)
SELF-CARE MORNING ROUTINE	□ SHOWER / BRUSH TEETH □ DRESS / HAIR CHECK □ MAKE BED / TIDY ROOM □ BREAKFAST	□ SHOWER / BRUSH TEETH □ DRESS / HAIR CHECK □ MAKE BED / TIDY ROOM □ BREAKFAST	□ SHOWER / BRUSH TEETH □ DRESS / HAIR CHECK □ MAKE BED / TIDY ROOM □ BREAKFAST	□ SHOWER / BRUSH TEETH □ DRESS / HAIR CHECK □ MAKE BED / TIDY ROOM □ BREAKFAST
TIME	6 AM 7 AM 8 AM 9 AM 10 AM 11 AM 12 PM 1 PM 2 PM 3 PM 4 PM 5 PM 6 PM 7 PM 8 PM 9 PM 10 PM 11 PM 12 AM	6 AM 7 AM 8 AM 9 AM 10 AM 11 AM 12 PM 1 PM 2 PM 3 PM 4 PM 5 PM 6 PM 7 PM 8 PM 9 PM 10 PM 11 PM 12 AM	6 AM 7 AM 8 AM 9 AM 10 AM 11 AM 12 PM 1 PM 2 PM 3 PM 4 PM 5 PM 6 PM 7 PM 8 PM 9 PM 10P M 11 PM 12 AM	6 AM 7 AM 8 AM 9 AM 10 AM 11 AM 12 PM 1 PM 2 PM 3 PM 4 PM 5 PM 6 PM 7 PM 8 PM 9 PM 10 PM 11 PM 12 AM
	MEAL	MEAL	MEAL	MEAL

S.L.E.E.P BEDTIME ROUTINE

ACTIVITIES FOR THE WEEK

BIBLE VERSE OF THE WEEK _____

FRIDAY	**SATURDAY**	**SUNDAY**	
			PRAY & HUSTLE, HUSTLE & PRAY DAYTIME ROUTINE
☐ WAKE (TIME)	☐ WAKE (TIME)	☐ WAKE (TIME)	
☐ WORSHIP	☐ WORSHIP	☐ WORSHIP	
☐ WORKOUT (TIME)	☐ WORKOUT (TIME)	☐ WORKOUT (TIME)	
☐ WATER (#BOTTLES)	☐ WATER (#BOTTLES)	☐ WATER (#BOTTLES)	

FRIDAY	SATURDAY	SUNDAY
☐ SHOWER / BRUSH TEETH	☐ SHOWER / BRUSH TEETH	☐ SHOWER / BRUSH TEETH
☐ DRESS / HAIR CHECK	☐ DRESS / HAIR CHECK	☐ DRESS / HAIR CHECK
☐ MAKE BED / TIDY ROOM	☐ MAKE BED / TIDY ROOM	☐ MAKE BED / TIDY ROOM
☐ BREAKFAST	☐ BREAKFAST	☐ BREAKFAST

FRIDAY	SATURDAY	SUNDAY
6 AM	6 AM	6 AM
7 AM	7 AM	7 AM
8 AM	8 AM	8 AM
9 AM	9 AM	9 AM
10 AM	10 AM	10 AM
11 AM	11 AM	11 AM
12 PM	12 PM	12 PM
1 PM	1 PM	1 PM
2 PM	2 PM	2 PM
3 PM	3 PM	3 PM
4 PM	4 PM	4 PM
5 PM	5 PM	5 PM
6 PM	6 PM	6 PM
7 PM	7 PM	7 PM
8 PM	8 PM	8 PM
9 PM	9 PM	9 PM
10 PM	10 PM	10 PM
11 PM	11 PM	11 PM
12 AM	12 AM	12 AM

REMINDERS / NOTES

MEAL	MEAL	MEAL

S.L.E.E.P BEDTIME ROUTINE

ACTIVITIES FOR THE WEEK

HAPPY THOUGHTS

	MONDAY	TUESDAY	WEDNESDAY	THURSDAY
4 W's WAKE ROUTINE	□ WAKE (TIME) ___ □ WORSHIP ___ □ WORKOUT (TIME) ___ □ WATER (#BOTTLES) ___	□ WAKE (TIME) ___ □ WORSHIP ___ □ WORKOUT (TIME) ___ □ WATER (#BOTTLES) ___	□ WAKE (TIME) ___ □ WORSHIP ___ □ WORKOUT (TIME) ___ □ WATER (#BOTTLES) ___	□ WAKE (TIME) ___ □ WORSHIP ___ □ WORKOUT (TIME) ___ □ WATER (#BOTTLES) ___
SELF-CARE MORNING ROUTINE	□ SHOWER / BRUSH TEETH □ DRESS / HAIR CHECK □ MAKE BED / TIDY ROOM □ BREAKFAST	□ SHOWER / BRUSH TEETH □ DRESS / HAIR CHECK □ MAKE BED / TIDY ROOM □ BREAKFAST	□ SHOWER / BRUSH TEETH □ DRESS / HAIR CHECK □ MAKE BED / TIDY ROOM □ BREAKFAST	□ SHOWER / BRUSH TEETH □ DRESS / HAIR CHECK □ MAKE BED / TIDY ROOM □ BREAKFAST
TIME	6 AM 7 AM 8 AM 9 AM 10 AM 11 AM 12 PM 1 PM 2 PM 3 PM 4 PM 5 PM 6 PM 7 PM 8 PM 9 PM 10 PM 11 PM 12 AM	6 AM 7 AM 8 AM 9 AM 10 AM 11 AM 12 PM 1 PM 2 PM 3 PM 4 PM 5 PM 6 PM 7 PM 8 PM 9 PM 10 PM 11 PM 12 AM	6 AM 7 AM 8 AM 9 AM 10 AM 11 AM 12 PM 1 PM 2 PM 3 PM 4 PM 5 PM 6 PM 7 PM 8 PM 9 PM 10P M 11 PM 12 AM	6 AM 7 AM 8 AM 9 AM 10 AM 11 AM 12 PM 1 PM 2 PM 3 PM 4 PM 5 PM 6 PM 7 PM 8 PM 9 PM 10 PM 11 PM 12 AM
	MEAL	**MEAL**	**MEAL**	**MEAL**
	_____	_____	_____	_____

S.L.E.E.P BEDTIME ROUTINE

_____ _____ _____ _____

_____ _____ _____ _____

ACTIVITIES FOR THE WEEK

_____ _____ _____ _____

BIBLE VERSE OF THE WEEK _____

FRIDAY	SATURDAY	SUNDAY

PRAY & HUSTLE, HUSTLE & PRAY DAYTIME ROUTINE

FRIDAY

☐ WAKE (TIME)
☐ WORSHIP
☐ WORKOUT (TIME)
☐ WATER (#BOTTLES)

☐ SHOWER / BRUSH TEETH
☐ DRESS / HAIR CHECK
☐ MAKE BED / TIDY ROOM
☐ BREAKFAST

SATURDAY

☐ WAKE (TIME)
☐ WORSHIP
☐ WORKOUT (TIME)
☐ WATER (#BOTTLES)

☐ SHOWER / BRUSH TEETH
☐ DRESS / HAIR CHECK
☐ MAKE BED / TIDY ROOM
☐ BREAKFAST

SUNDAY

☐ WAKE (TIME)
☐ WORSHIP
☐ WORKOUT (TIME)
☐ WATER (#BOTTLES)

☐ SHOWER / BRUSH TEETH
☐ DRESS / HAIR CHECK
☐ MAKE BED / TIDY ROOM
☐ BREAKFAST

FRIDAY	SATURDAY	SUNDAY
6 AM	6 AM	6 AM
7 AM	7 AM	7 AM
8 AM	8 AM	8 AM
9 AM	9 AM	9 AM
10 AM	10 AM	10 AM
11 AM	11 AM	11 AM
12 PM	12 PM	12 PM
1 PM	1 PM	1 PM
2 PM	2 PM	2 PM
3 PM	3 PM	3 PM
4 PM	4 PM	4 PM
5 PM	5 PM	5 PM
6 PM	6 PM	6 PM
7 PM	7 PM	7 PM
8 PM	8 PM	8 PM
9 PM	9 PM	9 PM
10 PM	10 PM	10 PM
11 PM	11 PM	11 PM
12 AM	12 AM	12 AM

REMINDERS / NOTES

MEAL   **MEAL**   **MEAL**

S.L.E.E.P BEDTIME ROUTINE

HAPPY THOUGHTS

ACTIVITIES FOR THE WEEK

MONTH	_____		

	MONDAY	**TUESDAY**	**WEDNESDAY**	**THURSDAY**
4 W's WAKE ROUTINE	□ WAKE (TIME) □ WORSHIP □ WORKOUT (TIME) □ WATER (#BOTTLES)	□ WAKE (TIME) □ WORSHIP □ WORKOUT (TIME) □ WATER (#BOTTLES)	□ WAKE (TIME) □ WORSHIP □ WORKOUT (TIME) □ WATER (#BOTTLES)	□ WAKE (TIME) □ WORSHIP □ WORKOUT (TIME) □ WATER (#BOTTLES)
SELF-CARE MORNING ROUTINE	□ SHOWER / BRUSH TEETH □ DRESS / HAIR CHECK □ MAKE BED / TIDY ROOM □ BREAKFAST	□ SHOWER / BRUSH TEETH □ DRESS / HAIR CHECK □ MAKE BED / TIDY ROOM □ BREAKFAST	□ SHOWER / BRUSH TEETH □ DRESS / HAIR CHECK □ MAKE BED / TIDY ROOM □ BREAKFAST	□ SHOWER / BRUSH TEETH □ DRESS / HAIR CHECK □ MAKE BED / TIDY ROOM □ BREAKFAST
TIME	6 AM 7 AM 8 AM 9 AM 10 AM 11 AM 12 PM 1 PM 2 PM 3 PM 4 PM 5 PM 6 PM 7 PM 8 PM 9 PM 10 PM 11 PM 12 AM	6 AM 7 AM 8 AM 9 AM 10 AM 11 AM 12 PM 1 PM 2 PM 3 PM 4 PM 5 PM 6 PM 7 PM 8 PM 9 PM 10 PM 11 PM 12 AM	6 AM 7 AM 8 AM 9 AM 10 AM 11 AM 12 PM 1 PM 2 PM 3 PM 4 PM 5 PM 6 PM 7 PM 8 PM 9 PM 10P M 11 PM 12 AM	6 AM 7 AM 8 AM 9 AM 10 AM 11 AM 12 PM 1 PM 2 PM 3 PM 4 PM 5 PM 6 PM 7 PM 8 PM 9 PM 10 PM 11 PM 12 AM
	MEAL	**MEAL**	**MEAL**	**MEAL**

S.L.E.E.P BEDTIME ROUTINE

ACTIVITIES FOR THE WEEK

BIBLE VERSE OF THE WEEK _____

FRIDAY	**SATURDAY**	**SUNDAY**	**PRAY & HUSTLE, HUSTLE & PRAY DAYTIME ROUTINE**

☐ WAKE (TIME) ___ | ☐ WAKE (TIME) ___ | ☐ WAKE (TIME) ___

☐ WORSHIP ___ | ☐ WORSHIP ___ | ☐ WORSHIP ___

☐ WORKOUT (TIME) ___ | ☐ WORKOUT (TIME) ___ | ☐ WORKOUT (TIME) ___

☐ WATER (#BOTTLES) ___ | ☐ WATER (#BOTTLES) ___ | ☐ WATER (#BOTTLES) ___

☐ SHOWER / BRUSH TEETH | ☐ SHOWER / BRUSH TEETH | ☐ SHOWER / BRUSH TEETH

☐ DRESS / HAIR CHECK | ☐ DRESS / HAIR CHECK | ☐ DRESS / HAIR CHECK

☐ MAKE BED / TIDY ROOM | ☐ MAKE BED / TIDY ROOM | ☐ MAKE BED / TIDY ROOM

☐ BREAKFAST | ☐ BREAKFAST | ☐ BREAKFAST

FRIDAY	SATURDAY	SUNDAY
6 AM	6 AM	6 AM
7 AM	7 AM	7 AM
8 AM	8 AM	8 AM
9 AM	9 AM	9 AM
10 AM	10 AM	10 AM
11 AM	11 AM	11 AM
12 PM	12 PM	12 PM
1 PM	1 PM	1 PM
2 PM	2 PM	2 PM
3 PM	3 PM	3 PM
4 PM	4 PM	4 PM
5 PM	5 PM	5 PM
6 PM	6 PM	6 PM
7 PM	7 PM	7 PM
8 PM	8 PM	8 PM
9 PM	9 PM	9 PM
10 PM	10 PM	10 PM
11 PM	11 PM	11 PM
12 AM	12 AM	12 AM

REMINDERS / NOTES

MEAL   MEAL   MEAL

S.L.E.E.P BEDTIME ROUTINE

HAPPY THOUGHTS

ACTIVITIES FOR THE WEEK

	MONDAY	TUESDAY	WEDNESDAY	THURSDAY
4 W's WAKE ROUTINE	☐ WAKE (TIME)	☐ WAKE (TIME)	☐ WAKE (TIME)	☐ WAKE (TIME)
	☐ WORSHIP	☐ WORSHIP	☐ WORSHIP	☐ WORSHIP
	☐ WORKOUT (TIME)	☐ WORKOUT (TIME)	☐ WORKOUT (TIME)	☐ WORKOUT (TIME)
	☐ WATER (#BOTTLES)	☐ WATER (#BOTTLES)	☐ WATER (#BOTTLES)	☐ WATER (#BOTTLES)
SELF-CARE MORNING ROUTINE	☐ SHOWER / BRUSH TEETH	☐ SHOWER / BRUSH TEETH	☐ SHOWER / BRUSH TEETH	☐ SHOWER / BRUSH TEETH
	☐ DRESS / HAIR CHECK	☐ DRESS / HAIR CHECK	☐ DRESS / HAIR CHECK	☐ DRESS / HAIR CHECK
	☐ MAKE BED / TIDY ROOM	☐ MAKE BED / TIDY ROOM	☐ MAKE BED / TIDY ROOM	☐ MAKE BED / TIDY ROOM
	☐ BREAKFAST	☐ BREAKFAST	☐ BREAKFAST	☐ BREAKFAST
TIME	6 AM	6 AM	6 AM	6 AM
	7 AM	7 AM	7 AM	7 AM
	8 AM	8 AM	8 AM	8 AM
	9 AM	9 AM	9 AM	9 AM
	10 AM	10 AM	10 AM	10 AM
	11 AM	11 AM	11 AM	11 AM
	12 PM	12 PM	12 PM	12 PM
	1 PM	1 PM	1 PM	1 PM
	2 PM	2 PM	2 PM	2 PM
	3 PM	3 PM	3 PM	3 PM
	4 PM	4 PM	4 PM	4 PM
	5 PM	5 PM	5 PM	5 PM
	6 PM	6 PM	6 PM	6 PM
	7 PM	7 PM	7 PM	7 PM
	8 PM	8 PM	8 PM	8 PM
	9 PM	9 PM	9 PM	9 PM
	10 PM	10 PM	10P M	10 PM
	11 PM	11 PM	11 PM	11 PM
	12 AM	12 AM	12 AM	12 AM
	MEAL	MEAL	MEAL	MEAL

S.L.E.E.P BEDTIME ROUTINE

ACTIVITIES FOR THE WEEK

BIBLE VERSE OF THE WEEK _____

FRIDAY	SATURDAY	SUNDAY	
			PRAY & HUSTLE, HUSTLE & PRAY DAYTIME ROUTINE
☐ WAKE (TIME)	☐ WAKE (TIME)	☐ WAKE (TIME)	
☐ WORSHIP	☐ WORSHIP	☐ WORSHIP	
☐ WORKOUT (TIME)	☐ WORKOUT (TIME)	☐ WORKOUT (TIME)	
☐ WATER (#BOTTLES)	☐ WATER (#BOTTLES)	☐ WATER (#BOTTLES)	
☐ SHOWER / BRUSH TEETH	☐ SHOWER / BRUSH TEETH	☐ SHOWER / BRUSH TEETH	
☐ DRESS / HAIR CHECK	☐ DRESS / HAIR CHECK	☐ DRESS / HAIR CHECK	
☐ MAKE BED / TIDY ROOM	☐ MAKE BED / TIDY ROOM	☐ MAKE BED / TIDY ROOM	
☐ BREAKFAST	☐ BREAKFAST	☐ BREAKFAST	

FRIDAY	SATURDAY	SUNDAY	
6 AM	6 AM	6 AM	
7 AM	7 AM	7 AM	
8 AM	8 AM	8 AM	
9 AM	9 AM	9 AM	**REMINDERS / NOTES**
10 AM	10 AM	10 AM	
11 AM	11 AM	11 AM	
12 PM	12 PM	12 PM	
1 PM	1 PM	1 PM	
2 PM	2 PM	2 PM	
3 PM	3 PM	3 PM	
4 PM	4 PM	4 PM	
5 PM	5 PM	5 PM	
6 PM	6 PM	6 PM	
7 PM	7 PM	7 PM	
8 PM	8 PM	8 PM	
9 PM	9 PM	9 PM	
10 PM	10 PM	10 PM	
11 PM	11 PM	11 PM	
12 AM	12 AM	12 AM	

MEAL	MEAL	MEAL

HAPPY THOUGHTS

S.L.E.E.P BEDTIME ROUTINE

ACTIVITIES FOR THE WEEK

	MONDAY	TUESDAY	WEDNESDAY	THURSDAY
4 W's WAKE ROUTINE	☐ WAKE (TIME) ☐ WORSHIP ☐ WORKOUT (TIME) ☐ WATER (#BOTTLES)	☐ WAKE (TIME) ☐ WORSHIP ☐ WORKOUT (TIME) ☐ WATER (#BOTTLES)	☐ WAKE (TIME) ☐ WORSHIP ☐ WORKOUT (TIME) ☐ WATER (#BOTTLES)	☐ WAKE (TIME) ☐ WORSHIP ☐ WORKOUT (TIME) ☐ WATER (#BOTTLES)
SELF-CARE MORNING ROUTINE	☐ SHOWER / BRUSH TEETH ☐ DRESS / HAIR CHECK ☐ MAKE BED / TIDY ROOM ☐ BREAKFAST	☐ SHOWER / BRUSH TEETH ☐ DRESS / HAIR CHECK ☐ MAKE BED / TIDY ROOM ☐ BREAKFAST	☐ SHOWER / BRUSH TEETH ☐ DRESS / HAIR CHECK ☐ MAKE BED / TIDY ROOM ☐ BREAKFAST	☐ SHOWER / BRUSH TEETH ☐ DRESS / HAIR CHECK ☐ MAKE BED / TIDY ROOM ☐ BREAKFAST
TIME	6 AM 7 AM 8 AM 9 AM 10 AM 11 AM 12 PM 1 PM 2 PM 3 PM 4 PM 5 PM 6 PM 7 PM 8 PM 9 PM 10 PM 11 PM 12 AM	6 AM 7 AM 8 AM 9 AM 10 AM 11 AM 12 PM 1 PM 2 PM 3 PM 4 PM 5 PM 6 PM 7 PM 8 PM 9 PM 10 PM 11 PM 12 AM	6 AM 7 AM 8 AM 9 AM 10 AM 11 AM 12 PM 1 PM 2 PM 3 PM 4 PM 5 PM 6 PM 7 PM 8 PM 9 PM 10P M 11 PM 12 AM	6 AM 7 AM 8 AM 9 AM 10 AM 11 AM 12 PM 1 PM 2 PM 3 PM 4 PM 5 PM 6 PM 7 PM 8 PM 9 PM 10 PM 11 PM 12 AM
	MEAL _____	MEAL _____	MEAL _____	MEAL _____

S.L.E.E.P BEDTIME ROUTINE

_____ _____ _____ _____

_____ _____ _____ _____

ACTIVITIES FOR THE WEEK

_____ _____ _____ _____

BIBLE VERSE OF THE WEEK _____

FRIDAY	SATURDAY	SUNDAY	
			PRAY & HUSTLE, HUSTLE & PRAY DAYTIME ROUTINE
☐ WAKE (TIME)	☐ WAKE (TIME)	☐ WAKE (TIME)	
☐ WORSHIP	☐ WORSHIP	☐ WORSHIP	
☐ WORKOUT (TIME)	☐ WORKOUT (TIME)	☐ WORKOUT (TIME)	
☐ WATER (#BOTTLES)	☐ WATER (#BOTTLES)	☐ WATER (#BOTTLES)	
☐ SHOWER / BRUSH TEETH	☐ SHOWER / BRUSH TEETH	☐ SHOWER / BRUSH TEETH	
☐ DRESS / HAIR CHECK	☐ DRESS / HAIR CHECK	☐ DRESS / HAIR CHECK	
☐ MAKE BED / TIDY ROOM	☐ MAKE BED / TIDY ROOM	☐ MAKE BED / TIDY ROOM	
☐ BREAKFAST	☐ BREAKFAST	☐ BREAKFAST	

FRIDAY	SATURDAY	SUNDAY	
6 AM	6 AM	6 AM	
7 AM	7 AM	7 AM	
8 AM	8 AM	8 AM	
9 AM	9 AM	9 AM	**REMINDERS / NOTES**
10 AM	10 AM	10 AM	
11 AM	11 AM	11 AM	
12 PM	12 PM	12 PM	
1 PM	1 PM	1 PM	
2 PM	2 PM	2 PM	
3 PM	3 PM	3 PM	
4 PM	4 PM	4 PM	
5 PM	5 PM	5 PM	
6 PM	6 PM	6 PM	
7 PM	7 PM	7 PM	
8 PM	8 PM	8 PM	
9 PM	9 PM	9 PM	
10 PM	10 PM	10 PM	
11 PM	11 PM	11 PM	
12 AM	12 AM	12 AM	

MEAL	MEAL	MEAL

HAPPY THOUGHTS

S.L.E.E.P BEDTIME ROUTINE

ACTIVITIES FOR THE WEEK

	MONDAY	TUESDAY	WEDNESDAY	THURSDAY
4 W's WAKE ROUTINE	☐ WAKE (TIME) _____ ☐ WORSHIP _____ ☐ WORKOUT (TIME) _____ ☐ WATER (#BOTTLES) _____	☐ WAKE (TIME) _____ ☐ WORSHIP _____ ☐ WORKOUT (TIME) _____ ☐ WATER (#BOTTLES) _____	☐ WAKE (TIME) _____ ☐ WORSHIP _____ ☐ WORKOUT (TIME) _____ ☐ WATER (#BOTTLES) _____	☐ WAKE (TIME) _____ ☐ WORSHIP _____ ☐ WORKOUT (TIME) _____ ☐ WATER (#BOTTLES) _____
SELF-CARE MORNING ROUTINE	☐ SHOWER / BRUSH TEETH ☐ DRESS / HAIR CHECK ☐ MAKE BED / TIDY ROOM ☐ BREAKFAST	☐ SHOWER / BRUSH TEETH ☐ DRESS / HAIR CHECK ☐ MAKE BED / TIDY ROOM ☐ BREAKFAST	☐ SHOWER / BRUSH TEETH ☐ DRESS / HAIR CHECK ☐ MAKE BED / TIDY ROOM ☐ BREAKFAST	☐ SHOWER / BRUSH TEETH ☐ DRESS / HAIR CHECK ☐ MAKE BED / TIDY ROOM ☐ BREAKFAST
TIME	6 AM 7 AM 8 AM 9 AM 10 AM 11 AM 12 PM 1 PM 2 PM 3 PM 4 PM 5 PM 6 PM 7 PM 8 PM 9 PM 10 PM 11 PM 12 AM	6 AM 7 AM 8 AM 9 AM 10 AM 11 AM 12 PM 1 PM 2 PM 3 PM 4 PM 5 PM 6 PM 7 PM 8 PM 9 PM 10 PM 11 PM 12 AM	6 AM 7 AM 8 AM 9 AM 10 AM 11 AM 12 PM 1 PM 2 PM 3 PM 4 PM 5 PM 6 PM 7 PM 8 PM 9 PM 10P M 11 PM 12 AM	6 AM 7 AM 8 AM 9 AM 10 AM 11 AM 12 PM 1 PM 2 PM 3 PM 4 PM 5 PM 6 PM 7 PM 8 PM 9 PM 10 PM 11 PM 12 AM
	MEAL _____	**MEAL** _____	**MEAL** _____	**MEAL** _____

S.L.E.E.P BEDTIME ROUTINE

_____ _____ _____ _____
_____ _____ _____ _____

ACTIVITIES FOR THE WEEK

_____ _____ _____ _____

BIBLE VERSE OF THE WEEK _____

FRIDAY

☐ WAKE (TIME) _____
☐ WORSHIP _____
☐ WORKOUT (TIME) _____
☐ WATER (#BOTTLES) _____

☐ SHOWER / BRUSH TEETH
☐ DRESS / HAIR CHECK
☐ MAKE BED / TIDY ROOM
☐ BREAKFAST

6 AM _____
7 AM _____
8 AM _____
9 AM _____
10 AM _____
11 AM _____
12 PM _____
1 PM _____
2 PM _____
3 PM _____
4 PM _____
5 PM _____
6 PM _____
7 PM _____
8 PM _____
9 PM _____
10 PM _____
11 PM _____
12 AM _____

SATURDAY

☐ WAKE (TIME) _____
☐ WORSHIP _____
☐ WORKOUT (TIME) _____
☐ WATER (#BOTTLES) _____

☐ SHOWER / BRUSH TEETH
☐ DRESS / HAIR CHECK
☐ MAKE BED / TIDY ROOM
☐ BREAKFAST

6 AM _____
7 AM _____
8 AM _____
9 AM _____
10 AM _____
11 AM _____
12 PM _____
1 PM _____
2 PM _____
3 PM _____
4 PM _____
5 PM _____
6 PM _____
7 PM _____
8 PM _____
9 PM _____
10 PM _____
11 PM _____
12 AM _____

SUNDAY

☐ WAKE (TIME) _____
☐ WORSHIP _____
☐ WORKOUT (TIME) _____
☐ WATER (#BOTTLES) _____

☐ SHOWER / BRUSH TEETH
☐ DRESS / HAIR CHECK
☐ MAKE BED / TIDY ROOM
☐ BREAKFAST

6 AM _____
7 AM _____
8 AM _____
9 AM _____
10 AM _____
11 AM _____
12 PM _____
1 PM _____
2 PM _____
3 PM _____
4 PM _____
5 PM _____
6 PM _____
7 PM _____
8 PM _____
9 PM _____
10 PM _____
11 PM _____
12 AM _____

PRAY & HUSTLE, HUSTLE & PRAY DAYTIME ROUTINE

_____
_____
_____
_____
_____
_____

REMINDERS / NOTES

_____
_____
_____
_____
_____
_____
_____
_____

MEAL   MEAL   MEAL
_____   _____   _____

S.L.E.E.P BEDTIME ROUTINE

_____   _____   _____
_____   _____   _____

HAPPY THOUGHTS
_____
_____
_____
_____
_____

ACTIVITIES FOR THE WEEK

_____   _____   _____

	MONDAY	TUESDAY	WEDNESDAY	THURSDAY
4 W's WAKE ROUTINE	□ WAKE (TIME) □ WORSHIP □ WORKOUT (TIME) □ WATER (#BOTTLES)	□ WAKE (TIME) □ WORSHIP □ WORKOUT (TIME) □ WATER (#BOTTLES)	□ WAKE (TIME) □ WORSHIP □ WORKOUT (TIME) □ WATER (#BOTTLES)	□ WAKE (TIME) □ WORSHIP □ WORKOUT (TIME) □ WATER (#BOTTLES)
SELF-CARE MORNING ROUTINE	□ SHOWER / BRUSH TEETH □ DRESS / HAIR CHECK □ MAKE BED / TIDY ROOM □ BREAKFAST	□ SHOWER / BRUSH TEETH □ DRESS / HAIR CHECK □ MAKE BED / TIDY ROOM □ BREAKFAST	□ SHOWER / BRUSH TEETH □ DRESS / HAIR CHECK □ MAKE BED / TIDY ROOM □ BREAKFAST	□ SHOWER / BRUSH TEETH □ DRESS / HAIR CHECK □ MAKE BED / TIDY ROOM □ BREAKFAST
TIME	6 AM 7 AM 8 AM 9 AM 10 AM 11 AM 12 PM 1 PM 2 PM 3 PM 4 PM 5 PM 6 PM 7 PM 8 PM 9 PM 10 PM 11 PM 12 AM	6 AM 7 AM 8 AM 9 AM 10 AM 11 AM 12 PM 1 PM 2 PM 3 PM 4 PM 5 PM 6 PM 7 PM 8 PM 9 PM 10 PM 11 PM 12 AM	6 AM 7 AM 8 AM 9 AM 10 AM 11 AM 12 PM 1 PM 2 PM 3 PM 4 PM 5 PM 6 PM 7 PM 8 PM 9 PM 10P M 11 PM 12 AM	6 AM 7 AM 8 AM 9 AM 10 AM 11 AM 12 PM 1 PM 2 PM 3 PM 4 PM 5 PM 6 PM 7 PM 8 PM 9 PM 10 PM 11 PM 12 AM
	MEAL	MEAL	MEAL	MEAL

S.L.E.E.P BEDTIME ROUTINE

ACTIVITIES FOR THE WEEK

BIBLE VERSE OF THE WEEK _____

FRIDAY	SATURDAY	SUNDAY

**PRAY & HUSTLE, HUSTLE & PRAY
DAYTIME ROUTINE**

☐ WAKE (TIME)   ☐ WAKE (TIME)   ☐ WAKE (TIME)

☐ WORSHIP   ☐ WORSHIP   ☐ WORSHIP

☐ WORKOUT (TIME)   ☐ WORKOUT (TIME)   ☐ WORKOUT (TIME)

☐ WATER (#BOTTLES)   ☐ WATER (#BOTTLES)   ☐ WATER (#BOTTLES)

☐ SHOWER / BRUSH TEETH   ☐ SHOWER / BRUSH TEETH   ☐ SHOWER / BRUSH TEETH

☐ DRESS / HAIR CHECK   ☐ DRESS / HAIR CHECK   ☐ DRESS / HAIR CHECK

☐ MAKE BED / TIDY ROOM   ☐ MAKE BED / TIDY ROOM   ☐ MAKE BED / TIDY ROOM

☐ BREAKFAST   ☐ BREAKFAST   ☐ BREAKFAST

FRIDAY	SATURDAY	SUNDAY
6 AM	6 AM	6 AM
7 AM	7 AM	7 AM
8 AM	8 AM	8 AM
9 AM	9 AM	9 AM
10 AM	10 AM	10 AM
11 AM	11 AM	11 AM
12 PM	12 PM	12 PM
1 PM	1 PM	1 PM
2 PM	2 PM	2 PM
3 PM	3 PM	3 PM
4 PM	4 PM	4 PM
5 PM	5 PM	5 PM
6 PM	6 PM	6 PM
7 PM	7 PM	7 PM
8 PM	8 PM	8 PM
9 PM	9 PM	9 PM
10 PM	10 PM	10 PM
11 PM	11 PM	11 PM
12 AM	12 AM	12 AM

REMINDERS / NOTES

     MEAL   MEAL   MEAL

HAPPY THOUGHTS

S.L.E.E.P BEDTIME ROUTINE

ACTIVITIES FOR THE WEEK

MONTH _____

	MONDAY	TUESDAY	WEDNESDAY	THURSDAY
4 W's WAKE ROUTINE	□ WAKE (TIME) □ WORSHIP □ WORKOUT (TIME) □ WATER (#BOTTLES)	□ WAKE (TIME) □ WORSHIP □ WORKOUT (TIME) □ WATER (#BOTTLES)	□ WAKE (TIME) □ WORSHIP □ WORKOUT (TIME) □ WATER (#BOTTLES)	□ WAKE (TIME) □ WORSHIP □ WORKOUT (TIME) □ WATER (#BOTTLES)
SELF-CARE MORNING ROUTINE	□ SHOWER / BRUSH TEETH □ DRESS / HAIR CHECK □ MAKE BED / TIDY ROOM □ BREAKFAST	□ SHOWER / BRUSH TEETH □ DRESS / HAIR CHECK □ MAKE BED / TIDY ROOM □ BREAKFAST	□ SHOWER / BRUSH TEETH □ DRESS / HAIR CHECK □ MAKE BED / TIDY ROOM □ BREAKFAST	□ SHOWER / BRUSH TEETH □ DRESS / HAIR CHECK □ MAKE BED / TIDY ROOM □ BREAKFAST
TIME	6 AM 7 AM 8 AM 9 AM 10 AM 11 AM 12 PM 1 PM 2 PM 3 PM 4 PM 5 PM 6 PM 7 PM 8 PM 9 PM 10 PM 11 PM 12 AM	6 AM 7 AM 8 AM 9 AM 10 AM 11 AM 12 PM 1 PM 2 PM 3 PM 4 PM 5 PM 6 PM 7 PM 8 PM 9 PM 10 PM 11 PM 12 AM	6 AM 7 AM 8 AM 9 AM 10 AM 11 AM 12 PM 1 PM 2 PM 3 PM 4 PM 5 PM 6 PM 7 PM 8 PM 9 PM 10P M 11 PM 12 AM	6 AM 7 AM 8 AM 9 AM 10 AM 11 AM 12 PM 1 PM 2 PM 3 PM 4 PM 5 PM 6 PM 7 PM 8 PM 9 PM 10 PM 11 PM 12 AM
	MEAL	MEAL	MEAL	MEAL

S.L.E.E.P BEDTIME ROUTINE

ACTIVITIES FOR THE WEEK

BIBLE VERSE OF THE WEEK _____

FRIDAY

- ☐ WAKE (TIME)
- ☐ WORSHIP
- ☐ WORKOUT (TIME)
- ☐ WATER (#BOTTLES)

- ☐ SHOWER / BRUSH TEETH
- ☐ DRESS / HAIR CHECK
- ☐ MAKE BED / TIDY ROOM
- ☐ BREAKFAST

SATURDAY

- ☐ WAKE (TIME)
- ☐ WORSHIP
- ☐ WORKOUT (TIME)
- ☐ WATER (#BOTTLES)

- ☐ SHOWER / BRUSH TEETH
- ☐ DRESS / HAIR CHECK
- ☐ MAKE BED / TIDY ROOM
- ☐ BREAKFAST

SUNDAY

- ☐ WAKE (TIME)
- ☐ WORSHIP
- ☐ WORKOUT (TIME)
- ☐ WATER (#BOTTLES)

- ☐ SHOWER / BRUSH TEETH
- ☐ DRESS / HAIR CHECK
- ☐ MAKE BED / TIDY ROOM
- ☐ BREAKFAST

PRAY & HUSTLE, HUSTLE & PRAY DAYTIME ROUTINE

FRIDAY	SATURDAY	SUNDAY
6 AM	6 AM	6 AM
7 AM	7 AM	7 AM
8 AM	8 AM	8 AM
9 AM	9 AM	9 AM
10 AM	10 AM	10 AM
11 AM	11 AM	11 AM
12 PM	12 PM	12 PM
1 PM	1 PM	1 PM
2 PM	2 PM	2 PM
3 PM	3 PM	3 PM
4 PM	4 PM	4 PM
5 PM	5 PM	5 PM
6 PM	6 PM	6 PM
7 PM	7 PM	7 PM
8 PM	8 PM	8 PM
9 PM	9 PM	9 PM
10 PM	10 PM	10 PM
11 PM	11 PM	11 PM
12 AM	12 AM	12 AM

REMINDERS / NOTES

MEAL   MEAL   MEAL

S.L.E.E.P BEDTIME ROUTINE

ACTIVITIES FOR THE WEEK

HAPPY THOUGHTS

MONTH _____

	MONDAY	TUESDAY	WEDNESDAY	THURSDAY
4 W's WAKE ROUTINE	☐ WAKE (TIME) _____ ☐ WORSHIP _____ ☐ WORKOUT (TIME) _____ ☐ WATER (#BOTTLES) _____	☐ WAKE (TIME) _____ ☐ WORSHIP _____ ☐ WORKOUT (TIME) _____ ☐ WATER (#BOTTLES) _____	☐ WAKE (TIME) _____ ☐ WORSHIP _____ ☐ WORKOUT (TIME) _____ ☐ WATER (#BOTTLES) _____	☐ WAKE (TIME) _____ ☐ WORSHIP _____ ☐ WORKOUT (TIME) _____ ☐ WATER (#BOTTLES) _____
SELF-CARE MORNING ROUTINE	☐ SHOWER / BRUSH TEETH ☐ DRESS / HAIR CHECK ☐ MAKE BED / TIDY ROOM ☐ BREAKFAST	☐ SHOWER / BRUSH TEETH ☐ DRESS / HAIR CHECK ☐ MAKE BED / TIDY ROOM ☐ BREAKFAST	☐ SHOWER / BRUSH TEETH ☐ DRESS / HAIR CHECK ☐ MAKE BED / TIDY ROOM ☐ BREAKFAST	☐ SHOWER / BRUSH TEETH ☐ DRESS / HAIR CHECK ☐ MAKE BED / TIDY ROOM ☐ BREAKFAST
TIME	6 AM 7 AM 8 AM 9 AM 10 AM 11 AM 12 PM 1 PM 2 PM 3 PM 4 PM 5 PM 6 PM 7 PM 8 PM 9 PM 10 PM 11 PM 12 AM	6 AM 7 AM 8 AM 9 AM 10 AM 11 AM 12 PM 1 PM 2 PM 3 PM 4 PM 5 PM 6 PM 7 PM 8 PM 9 PM 10 PM 11 PM 12 AM	6 AM 7 AM 8 AM 9 AM 10 AM 11 AM 12 PM 1 PM 2 PM 3 PM 4 PM 5 PM 6 PM 7 PM 8 PM 9 PM 10P M 11 PM 12 AM	6 AM 7 AM 8 AM 9 AM 10 AM 11 AM 12 PM 1 PM 2 PM 3 PM 4 PM 5 PM 6 PM 7 PM 8 PM 9 PM 10 PM 11 PM 12 AM
	MEAL _____	**MEAL** _____	**MEAL** _____	**MEAL** _____

S.L.E.E.P BEDTIME ROUTINE

_____ _____ _____ _____

_____ _____ _____ _____

ACTIVITIES FOR THE WEEK

_____ _____ _____ _____

BIBLE VERSE OF THE WEEK _____

FRIDAY	SATURDAY	SUNDAY	
			PRAY & HUSTLE, HUSTLE & PRAY DAYTIME ROUTINE
□ WAKE (TIME)	□ WAKE (TIME)	□ WAKE (TIME)	
□ WORSHIP	□ WORSHIP	□ WORSHIP	
□ WORKOUT (TIME)	□ WORKOUT (TIME)	□ WORKOUT (TIME)	
□ WATER (#BOTTLES)	□ WATER (#BOTTLES)	□ WATER (#BOTTLES)	
□ SHOWER / BRUSH TEETH	□ SHOWER / BRUSH TEETH	□ SHOWER / BRUSH TEETH	
□ DRESS / HAIR CHECK	□ DRESS / HAIR CHECK	□ DRESS / HAIR CHECK	
□ MAKE BED / TIDY ROOM	□ MAKE BED / TIDY ROOM	□ MAKE BED / TIDY ROOM	
□ BREAKFAST	□ BREAKFAST	□ BREAKFAST	

FRIDAY	SATURDAY	SUNDAY	
6 AM	6 AM	6 AM	
7 AM	7 AM	7 AM	
8 AM	8 AM	8 AM	
9 AM	9 AM	9 AM	**REMINDERS / NOTES**
10 AM	10 AM	10 AM	
11 AM	11 AM	11 AM	
12 PM	12 PM	12 PM	
1 PM	1 PM	1 PM	
2 PM	2 PM	2 PM	
3 PM	3 PM	3 PM	
4 PM	4 PM	4 PM	
5 PM	5 PM	5 PM	
6 PM	6 PM	6 PM	
7 PM	7 PM	7 PM	
8 PM	8 PM	8 PM	
9 PM	9 PM	9 PM	
10 PM	10 PM	10 PM	
11 PM	11 PM	11 PM	
12 AM	12 AM	12 AM	

MEAL	MEAL	MEAL

S.L.E.E.P BEDTIME ROUTINE

HAPPY THOUGHTS

ACTIVITIES FOR THE WEEK

MONTH _____

	MONDAY	TUESDAY	WEDNESDAY	THURSDAY
4 W's WAKE ROUTINE	□ WAKE (TIME) □ WORSHIP □ WORKOUT (TIME) □ WATER (#BOTTLES)	□ WAKE (TIME) □ WORSHIP □ WORKOUT (TIME) □ WATER (#BOTTLES)	□ WAKE (TIME) □ WORSHIP □ WORKOUT (TIME) □ WATER (#BOTTLES)	□ WAKE (TIME) □ WORSHIP □ WORKOUT (TIME) □ WATER (#BOTTLES)
SELF-CARE MORNING ROUTINE	□ SHOWER / BRUSH TEETH □ DRESS / HAIR CHECK □ MAKE BED / TIDY ROOM □ BREAKFAST	□ SHOWER / BRUSH TEETH □ DRESS / HAIR CHECK □ MAKE BED / TIDY ROOM □ BREAKFAST	□ SHOWER / BRUSH TEETH □ DRESS / HAIR CHECK □ MAKE BED / TIDY ROOM □ BREAKFAST	□ SHOWER / BRUSH TEETH □ DRESS / HAIR CHECK □ MAKE BED / TIDY ROOM □ BREAKFAST
TIME	6 AM 7 AM 8 AM 9 AM 10 AM 11 AM 12 PM 1 PM 2 PM 3 PM 4 PM 5 PM 6 PM 7 PM 8 PM 9 PM 10 PM 11 PM 12 AM	6 AM 7 AM 8 AM 9 AM 10 AM 11 AM 12 PM 1 PM 2 PM 3 PM 4 PM 5 PM 6 PM 7 PM 8 PM 9 PM 10 PM 11 PM 12 AM	6 AM 7 AM 8 AM 9 AM 10 AM 11 AM 12 PM 1 PM 2 PM 3 PM 4 PM 5 PM 6 PM 7 PM 8 PM 9 PM 10P M 11 PM 12 AM	6 AM 7 AM 8 AM 9 AM 10 AM 11 AM 12 PM 1 PM 2 PM 3 PM 4 PM 5 PM 6 PM 7 PM 8 PM 9 PM 10 PM 11 PM 12 AM
	MEAL	MEAL	MEAL	MEAL

S.L.E.E.P BEDTIME ROUTINE

ACTIVITIES FOR THE WEEK

BIBLE VERSE OF THE WEEK _____

FRIDAY

☐ WAKE (TIME) _____
☐ WORSHIP _____
☐ WORKOUT (TIME) _____
☐ WATER (#BOTTLES) _____

☐ SHOWER / BRUSH TEETH
☐ DRESS / HAIR CHECK
☐ MAKE BED / TIDY ROOM
☐ BREAKFAST

6 AM
7 AM
8 AM
9 AM
10 AM
11 AM
12 PM
1 PM
2 PM
3 PM
4 PM
5 PM
6 PM
7 PM
8 PM
9 PM
10 PM
11 PM
12 AM

MEAL

SATURDAY

☐ WAKE (TIME) _____
☐ WORSHIP _____
☐ WORKOUT (TIME) _____
☐ WATER (#BOTTLES) _____

☐ SHOWER / BRUSH TEETH
☐ DRESS / HAIR CHECK
☐ MAKE BED / TIDY ROOM
☐ BREAKFAST

6 AM
7 AM
8 AM
9 AM
10 AM
11 AM
12 PM
1 PM
2 PM
3 PM
4 PM
5 PM
6 PM
7 PM
8 PM
9 PM
10 PM
11 PM
12 AM

MEAL

SUNDAY

☐ WAKE (TIME) _____
☐ WORSHIP _____
☐ WORKOUT (TIME) _____
☐ WATER (#BOTTLES) _____

☐ SHOWER / BRUSH TEETH
☐ DRESS / HAIR CHECK
☐ MAKE BED / TIDY ROOM
☐ BREAKFAST

6 AM
7 AM
8 AM
9 AM
10 AM
11 AM
12 PM
1 PM
2 PM
3 PM
4 PM
5 PM
6 PM
7 PM
8 PM
9 PM
10 PM
11 PM
12 AM

MEAL

PRAY & HUSTLE, HUSTLE & PRAY DAYTIME ROUTINE

REMINDERS / NOTES

HAPPY THOUGHTS

S.L.E.E.P BEDTIME ROUTINE

ACTIVITIES FOR THE WEEK

	MONDAY	TUESDAY	WEDNESDAY	THURSDAY
4 W's WAKE ROUTINE	☐ WAKE (TIME) ☐ WORSHIP ☐ WORKOUT (TIME) ☐ WATER (#BOTTLES)	☐ WAKE (TIME) ☐ WORSHIP ☐ WORKOUT (TIME) ☐ WATER (#BOTTLES)	☐ WAKE (TIME) ☐ WORSHIP ☐ WORKOUT (TIME) ☐ WATER (#BOTTLES)	☐ WAKE (TIME) ☐ WORSHIP ☐ WORKOUT (TIME) ☐ WATER (#BOTTLES)
SELF-CARE MORNING ROUTINE	☐ SHOWER / BRUSH TEETH ☐ DRESS / HAIR CHECK ☐ MAKE BED / TIDY ROOM ☐ BREAKFAST	☐ SHOWER / BRUSH TEETH ☐ DRESS / HAIR CHECK ☐ MAKE BED / TIDY ROOM ☐ BREAKFAST	☐ SHOWER / BRUSH TEETH ☐ DRESS / HAIR CHECK ☐ MAKE BED / TIDY ROOM ☐ BREAKFAST	☐ SHOWER / BRUSH TEETH ☐ DRESS / HAIR CHECK ☐ MAKE BED / TIDY ROOM ☐ BREAKFAST
TIME	6 AM 7 AM 8 AM 9 AM 10 AM 11 AM 12 PM 1 PM 2 PM 3 PM 4 PM 5 PM 6 PM 7 PM 8 PM 9 PM 10 PM 11 PM 12 AM	6 AM 7 AM 8 AM 9 AM 10 AM 11 AM 12 PM 1 PM 2 PM 3 PM 4 PM 5 PM 6 PM 7 PM 8 PM 9 PM 10 PM 11 PM 12 AM	6 AM 7 AM 8 AM 9 AM 10 AM 11 AM 12 PM 1 PM 2 PM 3 PM 4 PM 5 PM 6 PM 7 PM 8 PM 9 PM 10P M 11 PM 12 AM	6 AM 7 AM 8 AM 9 AM 10 AM 11 AM 12 PM 1 PM 2 PM 3 PM 4 PM 5 PM 6 PM 7 PM 8 PM 9 PM 10 PM 11 PM 12 AM
	MEAL _____	**MEAL** _____	**MEAL** _____	**MEAL** _____

S.L.E.E.P BEDTIME ROUTINE

_____ _____ _____ _____

_____ _____ _____ _____

ACTIVITIES FOR THE WEEK

_____ _____ _____ _____

BIBLE VERSE OF THE WEEK _____

FRIDAY	SATURDAY	SUNDAY	
			PRAY & HUSTLE, HUSTLE & PRAY DAYTIME ROUTINE
☐ WAKE (TIME)	☐ WAKE (TIME)	☐ WAKE (TIME)	
☐ WORSHIP	☐ WORSHIP	☐ WORSHIP	
☐ WORKOUT (TIME)	☐ WORKOUT (TIME)	☐ WORKOUT (TIME)	
☐ WATER (#BOTTLES)	☐ WATER (#BOTTLES)	☐ WATER (#BOTTLES)	
☐ SHOWER / BRUSH TEETH	☐ SHOWER / BRUSH TEETH	☐ SHOWER / BRUSH TEETH	
☐ DRESS / HAIR CHECK	☐ DRESS / HAIR CHECK	☐ DRESS / HAIR CHECK	
☐ MAKE BED / TIDY ROOM	☐ MAKE BED / TIDY ROOM	☐ MAKE BED / TIDY ROOM	
☐ BREAKFAST	☐ BREAKFAST	☐ BREAKFAST	

FRIDAY	SATURDAY	SUNDAY	
6 AM	6 AM	6 AM	
7 AM	7 AM	7 AM	
8 AM	8 AM	8 AM	
9 AM	9 AM	9 AM	**REMINDERS / NOTES**
10 AM	10 AM	10 AM	
11 AM	11 AM	11 AM	
12 PM	12 PM	12 PM	
1 PM	1 PM	1 PM	
2 PM	2 PM	2 PM	
3 PM	3 PM	3 PM	
4 PM	4 PM	4 PM	
5 PM	5 PM	5 PM	
6 PM	6 PM	6 PM	
7 PM	7 PM	7 PM	
8 PM	8 PM	8 PM	
9 PM	9 PM	9 PM	
10 PM	10 PM	10 PM	
11 PM	11 PM	11 PM	
12 AM	12 AM	12 AM	

MEAL	MEAL	MEAL

HAPPY THOUGHTS

S.L.E.E.P BEDTIME ROUTINE

ACTIVITIES FOR THE WEEK

MONTH _____

	MONDAY	TUESDAY	WEDNESDAY	THURSDAY
4 W's WAKE ROUTINE	□ WAKE (TIME)	□ WAKE (TIME)	□ WAKE (TIME)	□ WAKE (TIME)
	□ WORSHIP	□ WORSHIP	□ WORSHIP	□ WORSHIP
	□ WORKOUT (TIME)	□ WORKOUT (TIME)	□ WORKOUT (TIME)	□ WORKOUT (TIME)
	□ WATER (#BOTTLES)	□ WATER (#BOTTLES)	□ WATER (#BOTTLES)	□ WATER (#BOTTLES)
SELF-CARE MORNING ROUTINE	□ SHOWER / BRUSH TEETH	□ SHOWER / BRUSH TEETH	□ SHOWER / BRUSH TEETH	□ SHOWER / BRUSH TEETH
	□ DRESS / HAIR CHECK	□ DRESS / HAIR CHECK	□ DRESS / HAIR CHECK	□ DRESS / HAIR CHECK
	□ MAKE BED / TIDY ROOM	□ MAKE BED / TIDY ROOM	□ MAKE BED / TIDY ROOM	□ MAKE BED / TIDY ROOM
	□ BREAKFAST	□ BREAKFAST	□ BREAKFAST	□ BREAKFAST
TIME	6 AM	6 AM	6 AM	6 AM
	7 AM	7 AM	7 AM	7 AM
	8 AM	8 AM	8 AM	8 AM
	9 AM	9 AM	9 AM	9 AM
	10 AM	10 AM	10 AM	10 AM
	11 AM	11 AM	11 AM	11 AM
	12 PM	12 PM	12 PM	12 PM
	1 PM	1 PM	1 PM	1 PM
	2 PM	2 PM	2 PM	2 PM
	3 PM	3 PM	3 PM	3 PM
	4 PM	4 PM	4 PM	4 PM
	5 PM	5 PM	5 PM	5 PM
	6 PM	6 PM	6 PM	6 PM
	7 PM	7 PM	7 PM	7 PM
	8 PM	8 PM	8 PM	8 PM
	9 PM	9 PM	9 PM	9 PM
	10 PM	10 PM	10P M	10 PM
	11 PM	11 PM	11 PM	11 PM
	12 AM	12 AM	12 AM	12 AM
	MEAL	**MEAL**	**MEAL**	**MEAL**

S.L.E.E.P BEDTIME ROUTINE

ACTIVITIES FOR THE WEEK

BIBLE VERSE OF THE WEEK _____

FRIDAY	SATURDAY	SUNDAY
☐ WAKE (TIME)	☐ WAKE (TIME)	☐ WAKE (TIME)
☐ WORSHIP	☐ WORSHIP	☐ WORSHIP
☐ WORKOUT (TIME)	☐ WORKOUT (TIME)	☐ WORKOUT (TIME)
☐ WATER (#BOTTLES)	☐ WATER (#BOTTLES)	☐ WATER (#BOTTLES)
☐ SHOWER / BRUSH TEETH	☐ SHOWER / BRUSH TEETH	☐ SHOWER / BRUSH TEETH
☐ DRESS / HAIR CHECK	☐ DRESS / HAIR CHECK	☐ DRESS / HAIR CHECK
☐ MAKE BED / TIDY ROOM	☐ MAKE BED / TIDY ROOM	☐ MAKE BED / TIDY ROOM
☐ BREAKFAST	☐ BREAKFAST	☐ BREAKFAST

PRAY & HUSTLE, HUSTLE & PRAY DAYTIME ROUTINE

FRIDAY	SATURDAY	SUNDAY
6 AM	6 AM	6 AM
7 AM	7 AM	7 AM
8 AM	8 AM	8 AM
9 AM	9 AM	9 AM
10 AM	10 AM	10 AM
11 AM	11 AM	11 AM
12 PM	12 PM	12 PM
1 PM	1 PM	1 PM
2 PM	2 PM	2 PM
3 PM	3 PM	3 PM
4 PM	4 PM	4 PM
5 PM	5 PM	5 PM
6 PM	6 PM	6 PM
7 PM	7 PM	7 PM
8 PM	8 PM	8 PM
9 PM	9 PM	9 PM
10 PM	10 PM	10 PM
11 PM	11 PM	11 PM
12 AM	12 AM	12 AM

REMINDERS / NOTES

MEAL	MEAL	MEAL

S.L.E.E.P BEDTIME ROUTINE

HAPPY THOUGHTS

ACTIVITIES FOR THE WEEK

MONTH _____

	MONDAY	TUESDAY	WEDNESDAY	THURSDAY
4 W's WAKE ROUTINE	☐ WAKE (TIME) ☐ WORSHIP ☐ WORKOUT (TIME) ☐ WATER (#BOTTLES)	☐ WAKE (TIME) ☐ WORSHIP ☐ WORKOUT (TIME) ☐ WATER (#BOTTLES)	☐ WAKE (TIME) ☐ WORSHIP ☐ WORKOUT (TIME) ☐ WATER (#BOTTLES)	☐ WAKE (TIME) ☐ WORSHIP ☐ WORKOUT (TIME) ☐ WATER (#BOTTLES)
SELF-CARE MORNING ROUTINE	☐ SHOWER / BRUSH TEETH ☐ DRESS / HAIR CHECK ☐ MAKE BED / TIDY ROOM ☐ BREAKFAST	☐ SHOWER / BRUSH TEETH ☐ DRESS / HAIR CHECK ☐ MAKE BED / TIDY ROOM ☐ BREAKFAST	☐ SHOWER / BRUSH TEETH ☐ DRESS / HAIR CHECK ☐ MAKE BED / TIDY ROOM ☐ BREAKFAST	☐ SHOWER / BRUSH TEETH ☐ DRESS / HAIR CHECK ☐ MAKE BED / TIDY ROOM ☐ BREAKFAST
TIME	6 AM 7 AM 8 AM 9 AM 10 AM 11 AM 12 PM 1 PM 2 PM 3 PM 4 PM 5 PM 6 PM 7 PM 8 PM 9 PM 10 PM 11 PM 12 AM	6 AM 7 AM 8 AM 9 AM 10 AM 11 AM 12 PM 1 PM 2 PM 3 PM 4 PM 5 PM 6 PM 7 PM 8 PM 9 PM 10 PM 11 PM 12 AM	6 AM 7 AM 8 AM 9 AM 10 AM 11 AM 12 PM 1 PM 2 PM 3 PM 4 PM 5 PM 6 PM 7 PM 8 PM 9 PM 10P M 11 PM 12 AM	6 AM 7 AM 8 AM 9 AM 10 AM 11 AM 12 PM 1 PM 2 PM 3 PM 4 PM 5 PM 6 PM 7 PM 8 PM 9 PM 10 PM 11 PM 12 AM
	MEAL _____	MEAL _____	MEAL _____	MEAL _____

S.L.E.E.P BEDTIME ROUTINE

_____ _____ _____ _____

_____ _____ _____ _____

ACTIVITIES FOR THE WEEK

_____ _____ _____ _____

BIBLE VERSE OF THE WEEK _____

FRIDAY	SATURDAY	SUNDAY	
			PRAY & HUSTLE, HUSTLE & PRAY DAYTIME ROUTINE
☐ WAKE (TIME)	☐ WAKE (TIME)	☐ WAKE (TIME)	
☐ WORSHIP	☐ WORSHIP	☐ WORSHIP	
☐ WORKOUT (TIME)	☐ WORKOUT (TIME)	☐ WORKOUT (TIME)	
☐ WATER (#BOTTLES)	☐ WATER (#BOTTLES)	☐ WATER (#BOTTLES)	
☐ SHOWER / BRUSH TEETH	☐ SHOWER / BRUSH TEETH	☐ SHOWER / BRUSH TEETH	
☐ DRESS / HAIR CHECK	☐ DRESS / HAIR CHECK	☐ DRESS / HAIR CHECK	
☐ MAKE BED / TIDY ROOM	☐ MAKE BED / TIDY ROOM	☐ MAKE BED / TIDY ROOM	
☐ BREAKFAST	☐ BREAKFAST	☐ BREAKFAST	

FRIDAY	SATURDAY	SUNDAY
6 AM	6 AM	6 AM
7 AM	7 AM	7 AM
8 AM	8 AM	8 AM
9 AM	9 AM	9 AM
10 AM	10 AM	10 AM
11 AM	11 AM	11 AM
12 PM	12 PM	12 PM
1 PM	1 PM	1 PM
2 PM	2 PM	2 PM
3 PM	3 PM	3 PM
4 PM	4 PM	4 PM
5 PM	5 PM	5 PM
6 PM	6 PM	6 PM
7 PM	7 PM	7 PM
8 PM	8 PM	8 PM
9 PM	9 PM	9 PM
10 PM	10 PM	10 PM
11 PM	11 PM	11 PM
12 AM	12 AM	12 AM

REMINDERS / NOTES

MEAL   MEAL   MEAL

S.L.E.E.P BEDTIME ROUTINE

HAPPY THOUGHTS

ACTIVITIES FOR THE WEEK

MONTH _____

	MONDAY	TUESDAY	WEDNESDAY	THURSDAY
4 W's WAKE ROUTINE	□ WAKE (TIME) □ WORSHIP □ WORKOUT (TIME) □ WATER (#BOTTLES)	□ WAKE (TIME) □ WORSHIP □ WORKOUT (TIME) □ WATER (#BOTTLES)	□ WAKE (TIME) □ WORSHIP □ WORKOUT (TIME) □ WATER (#BOTTLES)	□ WAKE (TIME) □ WORSHIP □ WORKOUT (TIME) □ WATER (#BOTTLES)
SELF-CARE MORNING ROUTINE	□ SHOWER / BRUSH TEETH □ DRESS / HAIR CHECK □ MAKE BED / TIDY ROOM □ BREAKFAST	□ SHOWER / BRUSH TEETH □ DRESS / HAIR CHECK □ MAKE BED / TIDY ROOM □ BREAKFAST	□ SHOWER / BRUSH TEETH □ DRESS / HAIR CHECK □ MAKE BED / TIDY ROOM □ BREAKFAST	□ SHOWER / BRUSH TEETH □ DRESS / HAIR CHECK □ MAKE BED / TIDY ROOM □ BREAKFAST
TIME	6 AM 7 AM 8 AM 9 AM 10 AM 11 AM 12 PM 1 PM 2 PM 3 PM 4 PM 5 PM 6 PM 7 PM 8 PM 9 PM 10 PM 11 PM 12 AM	6 AM 7 AM 8 AM 9 AM 10 AM 11 AM 12 PM 1 PM 2 PM 3 PM 4 PM 5 PM 6 PM 7 PM 8 PM 9 PM 10 PM 11 PM 12 AM	6 AM 7 AM 8 AM 9 AM 10 AM 11 AM 12 PM 1 PM 2 PM 3 PM 4 PM 5 PM 6 PM 7 PM 8 PM 9 PM 10P M 11 PM 12 AM	6 AM 7 AM 8 AM 9 AM 10 AM 11 AM 12 PM 1 PM 2 PM 3 PM 4 PM 5 PM 6 PM 7 PM 8 PM 9 PM 10 PM 11 PM 12 AM
	MEAL	**MEAL**	**MEAL**	**MEAL**

S.L.E.E.P BEDTIME ROUTINE

ACTIVITIES FOR THE WEEK

FRIDAY

☐ WAKE (TIME) _____
☐ WORSHIP
☐ WORKOUT (TIME) _____
☐ WATER (#BOTTLES) _____

☐ SHOWER / BRUSH TEETH
☐ DRESS / HAIR CHECK
☐ MAKE BED / TIDY ROOM
☐ BREAKFAST

6 AM
7 AM
8 AM
9 AM
10 AM
11 AM
12 PM
1 PM
2 PM
3 PM
4 PM
5 PM
6 PM
7 PM
8 PM
9 PM
10 PM
11 PM
12 AM

SATURDAY

☐ WAKE (TIME) _____
☐ WORSHIP
☐ WORKOUT (TIME) _____
☐ WATER (#BOTTLES) _____

☐ SHOWER / BRUSH TEETH
☐ DRESS / HAIR CHECK
☐ MAKE BED / TIDY ROOM
☐ BREAKFAST

6 AM
7 AM
8 AM
9 AM
10 AM
11 AM
12 PM
1 PM
2 PM
3 PM
4 PM
5 PM
6 PM
7 PM
8 PM
9 PM
10 PM
11 PM
12 AM

SUNDAY

☐ WAKE (TIME) _____
☐ WORSHIP
☐ WORKOUT (TIME) _____
☐ WATER (#BOTTLES) _____

☐ SHOWER / BRUSH TEETH
☐ DRESS / HAIR CHECK
☐ MAKE BED / TIDY ROOM
☐ BREAKFAST

6 AM
7 AM
8 AM
9 AM
10 AM
11 AM
12 PM
1 PM
2 PM
3 PM
4 PM
5 PM
6 PM
7 PM
8 PM
9 PM
10 PM
11 PM
12 AM

PRAY & HUSTLE, HUSTLE & PRAY DAYTIME ROUTINE

REMINDERS / NOTES

MEAL

MEAL

MEAL

S.L.E.E.P BEDTIME ROUTINE

HAPPY THOUGHTS

ACTIVITIES FOR THE WEEK

	MONDAY	TUESDAY	WEDNESDAY	THURSDAY
4 W's WAKE ROUTINE	□ WAKE (TIME) □ WORSHIP □ WORKOUT (TIME) □ WATER (#BOTTLES)	□ WAKE (TIME) □ WORSHIP □ WORKOUT (TIME) □ WATER (#BOTTLES)	□ WAKE (TIME) □ WORSHIP □ WORKOUT (TIME) □ WATER (#BOTTLES)	□ WAKE (TIME) □ WORSHIP □ WORKOUT (TIME) □ WATER (#BOTTLES)
SELF-CARE MORNING ROUTINE	□ SHOWER / BRUSH TEETH □ DRESS / HAIR CHECK □ MAKE BED / TIDY ROOM □ BREAKFAST	□ SHOWER / BRUSH TEETH □ DRESS / HAIR CHECK □ MAKE BED / TIDY ROOM □ BREAKFAST	□ SHOWER / BRUSH TEETH □ DRESS / HAIR CHECK □ MAKE BED / TIDY ROOM □ BREAKFAST	□ SHOWER / BRUSH TEETH □ DRESS / HAIR CHECK □ MAKE BED / TIDY ROOM □ BREAKFAST
TIME	6 AM 7 AM 8 AM 9 AM 10 AM 11 AM 12 PM 1 PM 2 PM 3 PM 4 PM 5 PM 6 PM 7 PM 8 PM 9 PM 10 PM 11 PM 12 AM	6 AM 7 AM 8 AM 9 AM 10 AM 11 AM 12 PM 1 PM 2 PM 3 PM 4 PM 5 PM 6 PM 7 PM 8 PM 9 PM 10 PM 11 PM 12 AM	6 AM 7 AM 8 AM 9 AM 10 AM 11 AM 12 PM 1 PM 2 PM 3 PM 4 PM 5 PM 6 PM 7 PM 8 PM 9 PM 10P M 11 PM 12 AM	6 AM 7 AM 8 AM 9 AM 10 AM 11 AM 12 PM 1 PM 2 PM 3 PM 4 PM 5 PM 6 PM 7 PM 8 PM 9 PM 10 PM 11 PM 12 AM
	MEAL	MEAL	MEAL	MEAL

S.L.E.E.P BEDTIME ROUTINE

ACTIVITIES FOR THE WEEK

BIBLE VERSE OF THE WEEK _____

FRIDAY	SATURDAY	SUNDAY	
			PRAY & HUSTLE, HUSTLE & PRAY DAYTIME ROUTINE
☐ WAKE (TIME)	☐ WAKE (TIME)	☐ WAKE (TIME)	
☐ WORSHIP	☐ WORSHIP	☐ WORSHIP	
☐ WORKOUT (TIME)	☐ WORKOUT (TIME)	☐ WORKOUT (TIME)	
☐ WATER (#BOTTLES)	☐ WATER (#BOTTLES)	☐ WATER (#BOTTLES)	
☐ SHOWER / BRUSH TEETH	☐ SHOWER / BRUSH TEETH	☐ SHOWER / BRUSH TEETH	
☐ DRESS / HAIR CHECK	☐ DRESS / HAIR CHECK	☐ DRESS / HAIR CHECK	
☐ MAKE BED / TIDY ROOM	☐ MAKE BED / TIDY ROOM	☐ MAKE BED / TIDY ROOM	
☐ BREAKFAST	☐ BREAKFAST	☐ BREAKFAST	

FRIDAY	SATURDAY	SUNDAY
6 AM	6 AM	6 AM
7 AM	7 AM	7 AM
8 AM	8 AM	8 AM
9 AM	9 AM	9 AM
10 AM	10 AM	10 AM
11 AM	11 AM	11 AM
12 PM	12 PM	12 PM
1 PM	1 PM	1 PM
2 PM	2 PM	2 PM
3 PM	3 PM	3 PM
4 PM	4 PM	4 PM
5 PM	5 PM	5 PM
6 PM	6 PM	6 PM
7 PM	7 PM	7 PM
8 PM	8 PM	8 PM
9 PM	9 PM	9 PM
10 PM	10 PM	10 PM
11 PM	11 PM	11 PM
12 AM	12 AM	12 AM

REMINDERS / NOTES

MEAL	MEAL	MEAL

S.L.E.E.P BEDTIME ROUTINE

ACTIVITIES FOR THE WEEK

HAPPY THOUGHTS

	MONDAY	TUESDAY	WEDNESDAY	THURSDAY
4 W's WAKE ROUTINE	□ WAKE (TIME) □ WORSHIP □ WORKOUT (TIME) □ WATER (#BOTTLES)	□ WAKE (TIME) □ WORSHIP □ WORKOUT (TIME) □ WATER (#BOTTLES)	□ WAKE (TIME) □ WORSHIP □ WORKOUT (TIME) □ WATER (#BOTTLES)	□ WAKE (TIME) □ WORSHIP □ WORKOUT (TIME) □ WATER (#BOTTLES)
SELF-CARE MORNING ROUTINE	□ SHOWER / BRUSH TEETH □ DRESS / HAIR CHECK □ MAKE BED / TIDY ROOM □ BREAKFAST	□ SHOWER / BRUSH TEETH □ DRESS / HAIR CHECK □ MAKE BED / TIDY ROOM □ BREAKFAST	□ SHOWER / BRUSH TEETH □ DRESS / HAIR CHECK □ MAKE BED / TIDY ROOM □ BREAKFAST	□ SHOWER / BRUSH TEETH □ DRESS / HAIR CHECK □ MAKE BED / TIDY ROOM □ BREAKFAST
TIME	6 AM 7 AM 8 AM 9 AM 10 AM 11 AM 12 PM 1 PM 2 PM 3 PM 4 PM 5 PM 6 PM 7 PM 8 PM 9 PM 10 PM 11 PM 12 AM	6 AM 7 AM 8 AM 9 AM 10 AM 11 AM 12 PM 1 PM 2 PM 3 PM 4 PM 5 PM 6 PM 7 PM 8 PM 9 PM 10 PM 11 PM 12 AM	6 AM 7 AM 8 AM 9 AM 10 AM 11 AM 12 PM 1 PM 2 PM 3 PM 4 PM 5 PM 6 PM 7 PM 8 PM 9 PM 10P M 11 PM 12 AM	6 AM 7 AM 8 AM 9 AM 10 AM 11 AM 12 PM 1 PM 2 PM 3 PM 4 PM 5 PM 6 PM 7 PM 8 PM 9 PM 10 PM 11 PM 12 AM
	MEAL	**MEAL**	**MEAL**	**MEAL**

S.L.E.E.P BEDTIME ROUTINE

ACTIVITIES FOR THE WEEK

BIBLE VERSE OF THE WEEK _____

FRIDAY

☐ WAKE (TIME) _____
☐ WORSHIP
☐ WORKOUT (TIME) _____
☐ WATER (#BOTTLES) _____

☐ SHOWER / BRUSH TEETH
☐ DRESS / HAIR CHECK
☐ MAKE BED / TIDY ROOM
☐ BREAKFAST

6 AM _____
7 AM _____
8 AM _____
9 AM _____
10 AM _____
11 AM _____
12 PM _____
1 PM _____
2 PM _____
3 PM _____
4 PM _____
5 PM _____
6 PM _____
7 PM _____
8 PM _____
9 PM _____
10 PM _____
11 PM _____
12 AM _____

MEAL
_____
_____
_____

SATURDAY

☐ WAKE (TIME) _____
☐ WORSHIP
☐ WORKOUT (TIME) _____
☐ WATER (#BOTTLES) _____

☐ SHOWER / BRUSH TEETH
☐ DRESS / HAIR CHECK
☐ MAKE BED / TIDY ROOM
☐ BREAKFAST

6 AM _____
7 AM _____
8 AM _____
9 AM _____
10 AM _____
11 AM _____
12 PM _____
1 PM _____
2 PM _____
3 PM _____
4 PM _____
5 PM _____
6 PM _____
7 PM _____
8 PM _____
9 PM _____
10 PM _____
11 PM _____
12 AM _____

MEAL

S.L.E.E.P BEDTIME ROUTINE
_____
_____

ACTIVITIES FOR THE WEEK
_____

SUNDAY

☐ WAKE (TIME) _____
☐ WORSHIP
☐ WORKOUT (TIME) _____
☐ WATER (#BOTTLES) _____

☐ SHOWER / BRUSH TEETH
☐ DRESS / HAIR CHECK
☐ MAKE BED / TIDY ROOM
☐ BREAKFAST

6 AM _____
7 AM _____
8 AM _____
9 AM _____
10 AM _____
11 AM _____
12 PM _____
1 PM _____
2 PM _____
3 PM _____
4 PM _____
5 PM _____
6 PM _____
7 PM _____
8 PM _____
9 PM _____
10 PM _____
11 PM _____
12 AM _____

MEAL
_____

PRAY & HUSTLE, HUSTLE & PRAY DAYTIME ROUTINE
_____
_____
_____
_____

REMINDERS / NOTES
_____
_____
_____
_____
_____
_____
_____

HAPPY THOUGHTS
_____
_____
_____
_____
_____

MONTH _____

	MONDAY	**TUESDAY**	**WEDNESDAY**	**THURSDAY**
4 W's WAKE ROUTINE	□ WAKE (TIME) □ WORSHIP □ WORKOUT (TIME) □ WATER (#BOTTLES)	□ WAKE (TIME) □ WORSHIP □ WORKOUT (TIME) □ WATER (#BOTTLES)	□ WAKE (TIME) □ WORSHIP □ WORKOUT (TIME) □ WATER (#BOTTLES)	□ WAKE (TIME) □ WORSHIP □ WORKOUT (TIME) □ WATER (#BOTTLES)
SELF-CARE MORNING ROUTINE	□ SHOWER / BRUSH TEETH □ DRESS / HAIR CHECK □ MAKE BED / TIDY ROOM □ BREAKFAST	□ SHOWER / BRUSH TEETH □ DRESS / HAIR CHECK □ MAKE BED / TIDY ROOM □ BREAKFAST	□ SHOWER / BRUSH TEETH □ DRESS / HAIR CHECK □ MAKE BED / TIDY ROOM □ BREAKFAST	□ SHOWER / BRUSH TEETH □ DRESS / HAIR CHECK □ MAKE BED / TIDY ROOM □ BREAKFAST
TIME	6 AM 7 AM 8 AM 9 AM 10 AM 11 AM 12 PM 1 PM 2 PM 3 PM 4 PM 5 PM 6 PM 7 PM 8 PM 9 PM 10 PM 11 PM 12 AM	6 AM 7 AM 8 AM 9 AM 10 AM 11 AM 12 PM 1 PM 2 PM 3 PM 4 PM 5 PM 6 PM 7 PM 8 PM 9 PM 10 PM 11 PM 12 AM	6 AM 7 AM 8 AM 9 AM 10 AM 11 AM 12 PM 1 PM 2 PM 3 PM 4 PM 5 PM 6 PM 7 PM 8 PM 9 PM 10P M 11 PM 12 AM	6 AM 7 AM 8 AM 9 AM 10 AM 11 AM 12 PM 1 PM 2 PM 3 PM 4 PM 5 PM 6 PM 7 PM 8 PM 9 PM 10 PM 11 PM 12 AM
	MEAL	**MEAL**	**MEAL**	**MEAL**

S.L.E.E.P BEDTIME ROUTINE

_____ _____ _____ _____

_____ _____ _____ _____

ACTIVITIES FOR THE WEEK

_____ _____ _____ _____

BIBLE VERSE OF THE WEEK _____

FRIDAY	SATURDAY	SUNDAY
□ WAKE (TIME)	□ WAKE (TIME)	□ WAKE (TIME)
□ WORSHIP	□ WORSHIP	□ WORSHIP
□ WORKOUT (TIME)	□ WORKOUT (TIME)	□ WORKOUT (TIME)
□ WATER (#BOTTLES)	□ WATER (#BOTTLES)	□ WATER (#BOTTLES)

PRAY & HUSTLE, HUSTLE & PRAY DAYTIME ROUTINE

FRIDAY	SATURDAY	SUNDAY
□ SHOWER / BRUSH TEETH	□ SHOWER / BRUSH TEETH	□ SHOWER / BRUSH TEETH
□ DRESS / HAIR CHECK	□ DRESS / HAIR CHECK	□ DRESS / HAIR CHECK
□ MAKE BED / TIDY ROOM	□ MAKE BED / TIDY ROOM	□ MAKE BED / TIDY ROOM
□ BREAKFAST	□ BREAKFAST	□ BREAKFAST

FRIDAY	SATURDAY	SUNDAY
6 AM	6 AM	6 AM
7 AM	7 AM	7 AM
8 AM	8 AM	8 AM
9 AM	9 AM	9 AM
10 AM	10 AM	10 AM
11 AM	11 AM	11 AM
12 PM	12 PM	12 PM
1 PM	1 PM	1 PM
2 PM	2 PM	2 PM
3 PM	3 PM	3 PM
4 PM	4 PM	4 PM
5 PM	5 PM	5 PM
6 PM	6 PM	6 PM
7 PM	7 PM	7 PM
8 PM	8 PM	8 PM
9 PM	9 PM	9 PM
10 PM	10 PM	10 PM
11 PM	11 PM	11 PM
12 AM	12 AM	12 AM

REMINDERS / NOTES

MEAL	MEAL	MEAL

S.L.E.E.P BEDTIME ROUTINE

HAPPY THOUGHTS

ACTIVITIES FOR THE WEEK

	MONDAY	TUESDAY	WEDNESDAY	THURSDAY
4 W's WAKE ROUTINE	☐ WAKE (TIME) ☐ WORSHIP ☐ WORKOUT (TIME) ☐ WATER (#BOTTLES)	☐ WAKE (TIME) ☐ WORSHIP ☐ WORKOUT (TIME) ☐ WATER (#BOTTLES)	☐ WAKE (TIME) ☐ WORSHIP ☐ WORKOUT (TIME) ☐ WATER (#BOTTLES)	☐ WAKE (TIME) ☐ WORSHIP ☐ WORKOUT (TIME) ☐ WATER (#BOTTLES)
SELF-CARE MORNING ROUTINE	☐ SHOWER / BRUSH TEETH ☐ DRESS / HAIR CHECK ☐ MAKE BED / TIDY ROOM ☐ BREAKFAST	☐ SHOWER / BRUSH TEETH ☐ DRESS / HAIR CHECK ☐ MAKE BED / TIDY ROOM ☐ BREAKFAST	☐ SHOWER / BRUSH TEETH ☐ DRESS / HAIR CHECK ☐ MAKE BED / TIDY ROOM ☐ BREAKFAST	☐ SHOWER / BRUSH TEETH ☐ DRESS / HAIR CHECK ☐ MAKE BED / TIDY ROOM ☐ BREAKFAST
TIME	6 AM 7 AM 8 AM 9 AM 10 AM 11 AM 12 PM 1 PM 2 PM 3 PM 4 PM 5 PM 6 PM 7 PM 8 PM 9 PM 10 PM 11 PM 12 AM	6 AM 7 AM 8 AM 9 AM 10 AM 11 AM 12 PM 1 PM 2 PM 3 PM 4 PM 5 PM 6 PM 7 PM 8 PM 9 PM 10 PM 11 PM 12 AM	6 AM 7 AM 8 AM 9 AM 10 AM 11 AM 12 PM 1 PM 2 PM 3 PM 4 PM 5 PM 6 PM 7 PM 8 PM 9 PM 10P M 11 PM 12 AM	6 AM 7 AM 8 AM 9 AM 10 AM 11 AM 12 PM 1 PM 2 PM 3 PM 4 PM 5 PM 6 PM 7 PM 8 PM 9 PM 10 PM 11 PM 12 AM
	MEAL	MEAL	MEAL	MEAL

S.L.E.E.P BEDTIME ROUTINE

ACTIVITIES FOR THE WEEK

BIBLE VERSE OF THE WEEK _____

FRIDAY

☐ WAKE (TIME) _____
☐ WORSHIP
☐ WORKOUT (TIME) _____
☐ WATER (#BOTTLES) _____

☐ SHOWER / BRUSH TEETH
☐ DRESS / HAIR CHECK
☐ MAKE BED / TIDY ROOM
☐ BREAKFAST

6 AM _____
7 AM _____
8 AM _____
9 AM _____
10 AM _____
11 AM _____
12 PM _____
1 PM _____
2 PM _____
3 PM _____
4 PM _____
5 PM _____
6 PM _____
7 PM _____
8 PM _____
9 PM _____
10 PM _____
11 PM _____
12 AM _____

MEAL

_____

SATURDAY

☐ WAKE (TIME) _____
☐ WORSHIP
☐ WORKOUT (TIME) _____
☐ WATER (#BOTTLES) _____

☐ SHOWER / BRUSH TEETH
☐ DRESS / HAIR CHECK
☐ MAKE BED / TIDY ROOM
☐ BREAKFAST

6 AM _____
7 AM _____
8 AM _____
9 AM _____
10 AM _____
11 AM _____
12 PM _____
1 PM _____
2 PM _____
3 PM _____
4 PM _____
5 PM _____
6 PM _____
7 PM _____
8 PM _____
9 PM _____
10 PM _____
11 PM _____
12 AM _____

MEAL

S.L.E.E.P BEDTIME ROUTINE

_____

SUNDAY

☐ WAKE (TIME) _____
☐ WORSHIP
☐ WORKOUT (TIME) _____
☐ WATER (#BOTTLES) _____

☐ SHOWER / BRUSH TEETH
☐ DRESS / HAIR CHECK
☐ MAKE BED / TIDY ROOM
☐ BREAKFAST

6 AM _____
7 AM _____
8 AM _____
9 AM _____
10 AM _____
11 AM _____
12 PM _____
1 PM _____
2 PM _____
3 PM _____
4 PM _____
5 PM _____
6 PM _____
7 PM _____
8 PM _____
9 PM _____
10 PM _____
11 PM _____
12 AM _____

MEAL

_____

ACTIVITIES FOR THE WEEK

_____

PRAY & HUSTLE, HUSTLE & PRAY DAYTIME ROUTINE

_____
_____
_____
_____

REMINDERS / NOTES

_____
_____
_____
_____
_____
_____

HAPPY THOUGHTS

_____
_____
_____
_____
_____

MONTH _____

	MONDAY	TUESDAY	WEDNESDAY	THURSDAY
4 W's WAKE ROUTINE	□ WAKE (TIME) □ WORSHIP □ WORKOUT (TIME) □ WATER (#BOTTLES)	□ WAKE (TIME) □ WORSHIP □ WORKOUT (TIME) □ WATER (#BOTTLES)	□ WAKE (TIME) □ WORSHIP □ WORKOUT (TIME) □ WATER (#BOTTLES)	□ WAKE (TIME) □ WORSHIP □ WORKOUT (TIME) □ WATER (#BOTTLES)
SELF-CARE MORNING ROUTINE	□ SHOWER / BRUSH TEETH □ DRESS / HAIR CHECK □ MAKE BED / TIDY ROOM □ BREAKFAST	□ SHOWER / BRUSH TEETH □ DRESS / HAIR CHECK □ MAKE BED / TIDY ROOM □ BREAKFAST	□ SHOWER / BRUSH TEETH □ DRESS / HAIR CHECK □ MAKE BED / TIDY ROOM □ BREAKFAST	□ SHOWER / BRUSH TEETH □ DRESS / HAIR CHECK □ MAKE BED / TIDY ROOM □ BREAKFAST
TIME	6 AM 7 AM 8 AM 9 AM 10 AM 11 AM 12 PM 1 PM 2 PM 3 PM 4 PM 5 PM 6 PM 7 PM 8 PM 9 PM 10 PM 11 PM 12 AM	6 AM 7 AM 8 AM 9 AM 10 AM 11 AM 12 PM 1 PM 2 PM 3 PM 4 PM 5 PM 6 PM 7 PM 8 PM 9 PM 10 PM 11 PM 12 AM	6 AM 7 AM 8 AM 9 AM 10 AM 11 AM 12 PM 1 PM 2 PM 3 PM 4 PM 5 PM 6 PM 7 PM 8 PM 9 PM 10P M 11 PM 12 AM	6 AM 7 AM 8 AM 9 AM 10 AM 11 AM 12 PM 1 PM 2 PM 3 PM 4 PM 5 PM 6 PM 7 PM 8 PM 9 PM 10 PM 11 PM 12 AM
	MEAL	MEAL	MEAL	MEAL

S.L.E.E.P BEDTIME ROUTINE

ACTIVITIES FOR THE WEEK

BIBLE VERSE OF THE WEEK _____

FRIDAY	SATURDAY	SUNDAY
□ WAKE (TIME)	□ WAKE (TIME)	□ WAKE (TIME)
□ WORSHIP	□ WORSHIP	□ WORSHIP
□ WORKOUT (TIME)	□ WORKOUT (TIME)	□ WORKOUT (TIME)
□ WATER (#BOTTLES)	□ WATER (#BOTTLES)	□ WATER (#BOTTLES)
□ SHOWER / BRUSH TEETH	□ SHOWER / BRUSH TEETH	□ SHOWER / BRUSH TEETH
□ DRESS / HAIR CHECK	□ DRESS / HAIR CHECK	□ DRESS / HAIR CHECK
□ MAKE BED / TIDY ROOM	□ MAKE BED / TIDY ROOM	□ MAKE BED / TIDY ROOM
□ BREAKFAST	□ BREAKFAST	□ BREAKFAST

PRAY & HUSTLE, HUSTLE & PRAY DAYTIME ROUTINE

FRIDAY	SATURDAY	SUNDAY
6 AM	6 AM	6 AM
7 AM	7 AM	7 AM
8 AM	8 AM	8 AM
9 AM	9 AM	9 AM
10 AM	10 AM	10 AM
11 AM	11 AM	11 AM
12 PM	12 PM	12 PM
1 PM	1 PM	1 PM
2 PM	2 PM	2 PM
3 PM	3 PM	3 PM
4 PM	4 PM	4 PM
5 PM	5 PM	5 PM
6 PM	6 PM	6 PM
7 PM	7 PM	7 PM
8 PM	8 PM	8 PM
9 PM	9 PM	9 PM
10 PM	10 PM	10 PM
11 PM	11 PM	11 PM
12 AM	12 AM	12 AM

REMINDERS / NOTES

MEAL	MEAL	MEAL

S.L.E.E.P BEDTIME ROUTINE

HAPPY THOUGHTS

ACTIVITIES FOR THE WEEK

MONTH _____

	MONDAY	TUESDAY	WEDNESDAY	THURSDAY
4 W's WAKE ROUTINE	☐ WAKE (TIME)	☐ WAKE (TIME)	☐ WAKE (TIME)	☐ WAKE (TIME)
	☐ WORSHIP	☐ WORSHIP	☐ WORSHIP	☐ WORSHIP
	☐ WORKOUT (TIME)	☐ WORKOUT (TIME)	☐ WORKOUT (TIME)	☐ WORKOUT (TIME)
	☐ WATER (#BOTTLES)	☐ WATER (#BOTTLES)	☐ WATER (#BOTTLES)	☐ WATER (#BOTTLES)
SELF-CARE MORNING ROUTINE	☐ SHOWER / BRUSH TEETH	☐ SHOWER / BRUSH TEETH	☐ SHOWER / BRUSH TEETH	☐ SHOWER / BRUSH TEETH
	☐ DRESS / HAIR CHECK	☐ DRESS / HAIR CHECK	☐ DRESS / HAIR CHECK	☐ DRESS / HAIR CHECK
	☐ MAKE BED / TIDY ROOM	☐ MAKE BED / TIDY ROOM	☐ MAKE BED / TIDY ROOM	☐ MAKE BED / TIDY ROOM
	☐ BREAKFAST	☐ BREAKFAST	☐ BREAKFAST	☐ BREAKFAST
TIME	6 AM	6 AM	6 AM	6 AM
	7 AM	7 AM	7 AM	7 AM
	8 AM	8 AM	8 AM	8 AM
	9 AM	9 AM	9 AM	9 AM
	10 AM	10 AM	10 AM	10 AM
	11 AM	11 AM	11 AM	11 AM
	12 PM	12 PM	12 PM	12 PM
	1 PM	1 PM	1 PM	1 PM
	2 PM	2 PM	2 PM	2 PM
	3 PM	3 PM	3 PM	3 PM
	4 PM	4 PM	4 PM	4 PM
	5 PM	5 PM	5 PM	5 PM
	6 PM	6 PM	6 PM	6 PM
	7 PM	7 PM	7 PM	7 PM
	8 PM	8 PM	8 PM	8 PM
	9 PM	9 PM	9 PM	9 PM
	10 PM	10 PM	10P M	10 PM
	11 PM	11 PM	11 PM	11 PM
	12 AM	12 AM	12 AM	12 AM
	MEAL	**MEAL**	**MEAL**	**MEAL**

S.L.E.E.P BEDTIME ROUTINE

ACTIVITIES FOR THE WEEK

BIBLE VERSE OF THE WEEK _____

FRIDAY

- ☐ WAKE (TIME) _____
- ☐ WORSHIP _____
- ☐ WORKOUT (TIME) _____
- ☐ WATER (#BOTTLES) _____

- ☐ SHOWER / BRUSH TEETH
- ☐ DRESS / HAIR CHECK
- ☐ MAKE BED / TIDY ROOM
- ☐ BREAKFAST

6 AM _____
7 AM _____
8 AM _____
9 AM _____
10 AM _____
11 AM _____
12 PM _____
1 PM _____
2 PM _____
3 PM _____
4 PM _____
5 PM _____
6 PM _____
7 PM _____
8 PM _____
9 PM _____
10 PM _____
11 PM _____
12 AM _____

SATURDAY

- ☐ WAKE (TIME) _____
- ☐ WORSHIP _____
- ☐ WORKOUT (TIME) _____
- ☐ WATER (#BOTTLES) _____

- ☐ SHOWER / BRUSH TEETH
- ☐ DRESS / HAIR CHECK
- ☐ MAKE BED / TIDY ROOM
- ☐ BREAKFAST

6 AM _____
7 AM _____
8 AM _____
9 AM _____
10 AM _____
11 AM _____
12 PM _____
1 PM _____
2 PM _____
3 PM _____
4 PM _____
5 PM _____
6 PM _____
7 PM _____
8 PM _____
9 PM _____
10 PM _____
11 PM _____
12 AM _____

SUNDAY

- ☐ WAKE (TIME) _____
- ☐ WORSHIP _____
- ☐ WORKOUT (TIME) _____
- ☐ WATER (#BOTTLES) _____

- ☐ SHOWER / BRUSH TEETH
- ☐ DRESS / HAIR CHECK
- ☐ MAKE BED / TIDY ROOM
- ☐ BREAKFAST

6 AM _____
7 AM _____
8 AM _____
9 AM _____
10 AM _____
11 AM _____
12 PM _____
1 PM _____
2 PM _____
3 PM _____
4 PM _____
5 PM _____
6 PM _____
7 PM _____
8 PM _____
9 PM _____
10 PM _____
11 PM _____
12 AM _____

PRAY & HUSTLE, HUSTLE & PRAY DAYTIME ROUTINE

_____
_____
_____
_____
_____
_____

REMINDERS / NOTES

_____
_____
_____
_____
_____
_____
_____

MEAL

MEAL

MEAL

S.L.E.E.P BEDTIME ROUTINE

ACTIVITIES FOR THE WEEK

HAPPY THOUGHTS
_____
_____
_____
_____
_____

MONTH			

	MONDAY	TUESDAY	WEDNESDAY	THURSDAY
4 W's WAKE ROUTINE	□ WAKE (TIME) □ WORSHIP □ WORKOUT (TIME) □ WATER (#BOTTLES)	□ WAKE (TIME) □ WORSHIP □ WORKOUT (TIME) □ WATER (#BOTTLES)	□ WAKE (TIME) □ WORSHIP □ WORKOUT (TIME) □ WATER (#BOTTLES)	□ WAKE (TIME) □ WORSHIP □ WORKOUT (TIME) □ WATER (#BOTTLES)
SELF-CARE MORNING ROUTINE	□ SHOWER / BRUSH TEETH □ DRESS / HAIR CHECK □ MAKE BED / TIDY ROOM □ BREAKFAST	□ SHOWER / BRUSH TEETH □ DRESS / HAIR CHECK □ MAKE BED / TIDY ROOM □ BREAKFAST	□ SHOWER / BRUSH TEETH □ DRESS / HAIR CHECK □ MAKE BED / TIDY ROOM □ BREAKFAST	□ SHOWER / BRUSH TEETH □ DRESS / HAIR CHECK □ MAKE BED / TIDY ROOM □ BREAKFAST
TIME	6 AM 7 AM 8 AM 9 AM 10 AM 11 AM 12 PM 1 PM 2 PM 3 PM 4 PM 5 PM 6 PM 7 PM 8 PM 9 PM 10 PM 11 PM 12 AM	6 AM 7 AM 8 AM 9 AM 10 AM 11 AM 12 PM 1 PM 2 PM 3 PM 4 PM 5 PM 6 PM 7 PM 8 PM 9 PM 10 PM 11 PM 12 AM	6 AM 7 AM 8 AM 9 AM 10 AM 11 AM 12 PM 1 PM 2 PM 3 PM 4 PM 5 PM 6 PM 7 PM 8 PM 9 PM 10P M 11 PM 12 AM	6 AM 7 AM 8 AM 9 AM 10 AM 11 AM 12 PM 1 PM 2 PM 3 PM 4 PM 5 PM 6 PM 7 PM 8 PM 9 PM 10 PM 11 PM 12 AM
	MEAL	MEAL	MEAL	MEAL

S.L.E.E.P BEDTIME ROUTINE

ACTIVITIES FOR THE WEEK

BIBLE VERSE OF THE WEEK _____

FRIDAY	SATURDAY	SUNDAY
□ WAKE (TIME)	□ WAKE (TIME)	□ WAKE (TIME)
□ WORSHIP	□ WORSHIP	□ WORSHIP
□ WORKOUT (TIME)	□ WORKOUT (TIME)	□ WORKOUT (TIME)
□ WATER (#BOTTLES)	□ WATER (#BOTTLES)	□ WATER (#BOTTLES)
□ SHOWER / BRUSH TEETH	□ SHOWER / BRUSH TEETH	□ SHOWER / BRUSH TEETH
□ DRESS / HAIR CHECK	□ DRESS / HAIR CHECK	□ DRESS / HAIR CHECK
□ MAKE BED / TIDY ROOM	□ MAKE BED / TIDY ROOM	□ MAKE BED / TIDY ROOM
□ BREAKFAST	□ BREAKFAST	□ BREAKFAST

PRAY & HUSTLE, HUSTLE & PRAY DAYTIME ROUTINE

FRIDAY	SATURDAY	SUNDAY
6 AM	6 AM	6 AM
7 AM	7 AM	7 AM
8 AM	8 AM	8 AM
9 AM	9 AM	9 AM
10 AM	10 AM	10 AM
11 AM	11 AM	11 AM
12 PM	12 PM	12 PM
1 PM	1 PM	1 PM
2 PM	2 PM	2 PM
3 PM	3 PM	3 PM
4 PM	4 PM	4 PM
5 PM	5 PM	5 PM
6 PM	6 PM	6 PM
7 PM	7 PM	7 PM
8 PM	8 PM	8 PM
9 PM	9 PM	9 PM
10 PM	10 PM	10 PM
11 PM	11 PM	11 PM
12 AM	12 AM	12 AM

REMINDERS / NOTES

MEAL	MEAL	MEAL

S.L.E.E.P BEDTIME ROUTINE

HAPPY THOUGHTS

ACTIVITIES FOR THE WEEK

	MONDAY	TUESDAY	WEDNESDAY	THURSDAY
4 W's WAKE ROUTINE	☐ WAKE (TIME) ☐ WORSHIP ☐ WORKOUT (TIME) ☐ WATER (#BOTTLES)	☐ WAKE (TIME) ☐ WORSHIP ☐ WORKOUT (TIME) ☐ WATER (#BOTTLES)	☐ WAKE (TIME) ☐ WORSHIP ☐ WORKOUT (TIME) ☐ WATER (#BOTTLES)	☐ WAKE (TIME) ☐ WORSHIP ☐ WORKOUT (TIME) ☐ WATER (#BOTTLES)
SELF-CARE MORNING ROUTINE	☐ SHOWER / BRUSH TEETH ☐ DRESS / HAIR CHECK ☐ MAKE BED / TIDY ROOM ☐ BREAKFAST	☐ SHOWER / BRUSH TEETH ☐ DRESS / HAIR CHECK ☐ MAKE BED / TIDY ROOM ☐ BREAKFAST	☐ SHOWER / BRUSH TEETH ☐ DRESS / HAIR CHECK ☐ MAKE BED / TIDY ROOM ☐ BREAKFAST	☐ SHOWER / BRUSH TEETH ☐ DRESS / HAIR CHECK ☐ MAKE BED / TIDY ROOM ☐ BREAKFAST
TIME	6 AM 7 AM 8 AM 9 AM 10 AM 11 AM 12 PM 1 PM 2 PM 3 PM 4 PM 5 PM 6 PM 7 PM 8 PM 9 PM 10 PM 11 PM 12 AM	6 AM 7 AM 8 AM 9 AM 10 AM 11 AM 12 PM 1 PM 2 PM 3 PM 4 PM 5 PM 6 PM 7 PM 8 PM 9 PM 10 PM 11 PM 12 AM	6 AM 7 AM 8 AM 9 AM 10 AM 11 AM 12 PM 1 PM 2 PM 3 PM 4 PM 5 PM 6 PM 7 PM 8 PM 9 PM 10P M 11 PM 12 AM	6 AM 7 AM 8 AM 9 AM 10 AM 11 AM 12 PM 1 PM 2 PM 3 PM 4 PM 5 PM 6 PM 7 PM 8 PM 9 PM 10 PM 11 PM 12 AM
	MEAL	**MEAL**	**MEAL**	**MEAL**

S.L.E.E.P BEDTIME ROUTINE

ACTIVITIES FOR THE WEEK

FRIDAY

☐ WAKE (TIME) _____
☐ WORSHIP _____
☐ WORKOUT (TIME) _____
☐ WATER (#BOTTLES) _____

☐ SHOWER / BRUSH TEETH
☐ DRESS / HAIR CHECK
☐ MAKE BED / TIDY ROOM
☐ BREAKFAST

6 AM _____
7 AM _____
8 AM _____
9 AM _____
10 AM _____
11 AM _____
12 PM _____
1 PM _____
2 PM _____
3 PM _____
4 PM _____
5 PM _____
6 PM _____
7 PM _____
8 PM _____
9 PM _____
10 PM _____
11 PM _____
12 AM _____

MEAL
_____
_____
_____
_____

SATURDAY

☐ WAKE (TIME) _____
☐ WORSHIP _____
☐ WORKOUT (TIME) _____
☐ WATER (#BOTTLES) _____

☐ SHOWER / BRUSH TEETH
☐ DRESS / HAIR CHECK
☐ MAKE BED / TIDY ROOM
☐ BREAKFAST

6 AM _____
7 AM _____
8 AM _____
9 AM _____
10 AM _____
11 AM _____
12 PM _____
1 PM _____
2 PM _____
3 PM _____
4 PM _____
5 PM _____
6 PM _____
7 PM _____
8 PM _____
9 PM _____
10 PM _____
11 PM _____
12 AM _____

MEAL
_____

S.L.E.E.P BEDTIME ROUTINE
_____
_____

ACTIVITIES FOR THE WEEK
_____

SUNDAY

☐ WAKE (TIME) _____
☐ WORSHIP _____
☐ WORKOUT (TIME) _____
☐ WATER (#BOTTLES) _____

☐ SHOWER / BRUSH TEETH
☐ DRESS / HAIR CHECK
☐ MAKE BED / TIDY ROOM
☐ BREAKFAST

6 AM _____
7 AM _____
8 AM _____
9 AM _____
10 AM _____
11 AM _____
12 PM _____
1 PM _____
2 PM _____
3 PM _____
4 PM _____
5 PM _____
6 PM _____
7 PM _____
8 PM _____
9 PM _____
10 PM _____
11 PM _____
12 AM _____

MEAL
_____
_____
_____
_____

PRAY & HUSTLE, HUSTLE & PRAY DAYTIME ROUTINE

_____
_____
_____
_____
_____

REMINDERS / NOTES

_____
_____
_____
_____
_____
_____
_____

HAPPY THOUGHTS

_____
_____
_____
_____
_____

	MONDAY	TUESDAY	WEDNESDAY	THURSDAY
4 W's WAKE ROUTINE	□ WAKE (TIME) □ WORSHIP □ WORKOUT (TIME) □ WATER (#BOTTLES)	□ WAKE (TIME) □ WORSHIP □ WORKOUT (TIME) □ WATER (#BOTTLES)	□ WAKE (TIME) □ WORSHIP □ WORKOUT (TIME) □ WATER (#BOTTLES)	□ WAKE (TIME) □ WORSHIP □ WORKOUT (TIME) □ WATER (#BOTTLES)
SELF-CARE MORNING ROUTINE	□ SHOWER / BRUSH TEETH □ DRESS / HAIR CHECK □ MAKE BED / TIDY ROOM □ BREAKFAST	□ SHOWER / BRUSH TEETH □ DRESS / HAIR CHECK □ MAKE BED / TIDY ROOM □ BREAKFAST	□ SHOWER / BRUSH TEETH □ DRESS / HAIR CHECK □ MAKE BED / TIDY ROOM □ BREAKFAST	□ SHOWER / BRUSH TEETH □ DRESS / HAIR CHECK □ MAKE BED / TIDY ROOM □ BREAKFAST
TIME	6 AM 7 AM 8 AM 9 AM 10 AM 11 AM 12 PM 1 PM 2 PM 3 PM 4 PM 5 PM 6 PM 7 PM 8 PM 9 PM 10 PM 11 PM 12 AM	6 AM 7 AM 8 AM 9 AM 10 AM 11 AM 12 PM 1 PM 2 PM 3 PM 4 PM 5 PM 6 PM 7 PM 8 PM 9 PM 10 PM 11 PM 12 AM	6 AM 7 AM 8 AM 9 AM 10 AM 11 AM 12 PM 1 PM 2 PM 3 PM 4 PM 5 PM 6 PM 7 PM 8 PM 9 PM 10P M 11 PM 12 AM	6 AM 7 AM 8 AM 9 AM 10 AM 11 AM 12 PM 1 PM 2 PM 3 PM 4 PM 5 PM 6 PM 7 PM 8 PM 9 PM 10 PM 11 PM 12 AM
	MEAL	MEAL	MEAL	MEAL

S.L.E.E.P BEDTIME ROUTINE

ACTIVITIES FOR THE WEEK

BIBLE VERSE OF THE WEEK _____

FRIDAY	SATURDAY	SUNDAY
□ WAKE (TIME)	□ WAKE (TIME)	□ WAKE (TIME)
□ WORSHIP	□ WORSHIP	□ WORSHIP
□ WORKOUT (TIME)	□ WORKOUT (TIME)	□ WORKOUT (TIME)
□ WATER (#BOTTLES)	□ WATER (#BOTTLES)	□ WATER (#BOTTLES)
□ SHOWER / BRUSH TEETH	□ SHOWER / BRUSH TEETH	□ SHOWER / BRUSH TEETH
□ DRESS / HAIR CHECK	□ DRESS / HAIR CHECK	□ DRESS / HAIR CHECK
□ MAKE BED / TIDY ROOM	□ MAKE BED / TIDY ROOM	□ MAKE BED / TIDY ROOM
□ BREAKFAST	□ BREAKFAST	□ BREAKFAST

PRAY & HUSTLE, HUSTLE & PRAY DAYTIME ROUTINE

FRIDAY	SATURDAY	SUNDAY
6 AM	6 AM	6 AM
7 AM	7 AM	7 AM
8 AM	8 AM	8 AM
9 AM	9 AM	9 AM
10 AM	10 AM	10 AM
11 AM	11 AM	11 AM
12 PM	12 PM	12 PM
1 PM	1 PM	1 PM
2 PM	2 PM	2 PM
3 PM	3 PM	3 PM
4 PM	4 PM	4 PM
5 PM	5 PM	5 PM
6 PM	6 PM	6 PM
7 PM	7 PM	7 PM
8 PM	8 PM	8 PM
9 PM	9 PM	9 PM
10 PM	10 PM	10 PM
11 PM	11 PM	11 PM
12 AM	12 AM	12 AM

REMINDERS / NOTES

MEAL	MEAL	MEAL

S.L.E.E.P BEDTIME ROUTINE

HAPPY THOUGHTS

ACTIVITIES FOR THE WEEK

MONTH _____

	MONDAY	TUESDAY	WEDNESDAY	THURSDAY
4 W's WAKE ROUTINE	☐ WAKE (TIME) ☐ WORSHIP ☐ WORKOUT (TIME) ☐ WATER (#BOTTLES)	☐ WAKE (TIME) ☐ WORSHIP ☐ WORKOUT (TIME) ☐ WATER (#BOTTLES)	☐ WAKE (TIME) ☐ WORSHIP ☐ WORKOUT (TIME) ☐ WATER (#BOTTLES)	☐ WAKE (TIME) ☐ WORSHIP ☐ WORKOUT (TIME) ☐ WATER (#BOTTLES)
SELF-CARE MORNING ROUTINE	☐ SHOWER / BRUSH TEETH ☐ DRESS / HAIR CHECK ☐ MAKE BED / TIDY ROOM ☐ BREAKFAST	☐ SHOWER / BRUSH TEETH ☐ DRESS / HAIR CHECK ☐ MAKE BED / TIDY ROOM ☐ BREAKFAST	☐ SHOWER / BRUSH TEETH ☐ DRESS / HAIR CHECK ☐ MAKE BED / TIDY ROOM ☐ BREAKFAST	☐ SHOWER / BRUSH TEETH ☐ DRESS / HAIR CHECK ☐ MAKE BED / TIDY ROOM ☐ BREAKFAST
TIME	6 AM 7 AM 8 AM 9 AM 10 AM 11 AM 12 PM 1 PM 2 PM 3 PM 4 PM 5 PM 6 PM 7 PM 8 PM 9 PM 10 PM 11 PM 12 AM	6 AM 7 AM 8 AM 9 AM 10 AM 11 AM 12 PM 1 PM 2 PM 3 PM 4 PM 5 PM 6 PM 7 PM 8 PM 9 PM 10 PM 11 PM 12 AM	6 AM 7 AM 8 AM 9 AM 10 AM 11 AM 12 PM 1 PM 2 PM 3 PM 4 PM 5 PM 6 PM 7 PM 8 PM 9 PM 10P M 11 PM 12 AM	6 AM 7 AM 8 AM 9 AM 10 AM 11 AM 12 PM 1 PM 2 PM 3 PM 4 PM 5 PM 6 PM 7 PM 8 PM 9 PM 10 PM 11 PM 12 AM
	MEAL	**MEAL**	**MEAL**	**MEAL**

S.L.E.E.P BEDTIME ROUTINE

ACTIVITIES FOR THE WEEK

FRIDAY	SATURDAY	SUNDAY	PRAY & HUSTLE, HUSTLE & PRAY DAYTIME ROUTINE
□ WAKE (TIME)	□ WAKE (TIME)	□ WAKE (TIME)	
□ WORSHIP	□ WORSHIP	□ WORSHIP	
□ WORKOUT (TIME)	□ WORKOUT (TIME)	□ WORKOUT (TIME)	
□ WATER (#BOTTLES)	□ WATER (#BOTTLES)	□ WATER (#BOTTLES)	
□ SHOWER / BRUSH TEETH	□ SHOWER / BRUSH TEETH	□ SHOWER / BRUSH TEETH	
□ DRESS / HAIR CHECK	□ DRESS / HAIR CHECK	□ DRESS / HAIR CHECK	
□ MAKE BED / TIDY ROOM	□ MAKE BED / TIDY ROOM	□ MAKE BED / TIDY ROOM	
□ BREAKFAST	□ BREAKFAST	□ BREAKFAST	

FRIDAY	SATURDAY	SUNDAY	
6 AM	6 AM	6 AM	
7 AM	7 AM	7 AM	
8 AM	8 AM	8 AM	
9 AM	9 AM	9 AM	REMINDERS / NOTES
10 AM	10 AM	10 AM	
11 AM	11 AM	11 AM	
12 PM	12 PM	12 PM	
1 PM	1 PM	1 PM	
2 PM	2 PM	2 PM	
3 PM	3 PM	3 PM	
4 PM	4 PM	4 PM	
5 PM	5 PM	5 PM	
6 PM	6 PM	6 PM	
7 PM	7 PM	7 PM	
8 PM	8 PM	8 PM	
9 PM	9 PM	9 PM	
10 PM	10 PM	10 PM	
11 PM	11 PM	11 PM	
12 AM	12 AM	12 AM	

MEAL	MEAL	MEAL	HAPPY THOUGHTS

S.L.E.E.P BEDTIME ROUTINE

ACTIVITIES FOR THE WEEK

	MONDAY	TUESDAY	WEDNESDAY	THURSDAY
4 W's WAKE ROUTINE	□ WAKE (TIME) □ WORSHIP □ WORKOUT (TIME) □ WATER (#BOTTLES)	□ WAKE (TIME) □ WORSHIP □ WORKOUT (TIME) □ WATER (#BOTTLES)	□ WAKE (TIME) □ WORSHIP □ WORKOUT (TIME) □ WATER (#BOTTLES)	□ WAKE (TIME) □ WORSHIP □ WORKOUT (TIME) □ WATER (#BOTTLES)
SELF-CARE MORNING ROUTINE	□ SHOWER / BRUSH TEETH □ DRESS / HAIR CHECK □ MAKE BED / TIDY ROOM □ BREAKFAST	□ SHOWER / BRUSH TEETH □ DRESS / HAIR CHECK □ MAKE BED / TIDY ROOM □ BREAKFAST	□ SHOWER / BRUSH TEETH □ DRESS / HAIR CHECK □ MAKE BED / TIDY ROOM □ BREAKFAST	□ SHOWER / BRUSH TEETH □ DRESS / HAIR CHECK □ MAKE BED / TIDY ROOM □ BREAKFAST
TIME	6 AM 7 AM 8 AM 9 AM 10 AM 11 AM 12 PM 1 PM 2 PM 3 PM 4 PM 5 PM 6 PM 7 PM 8 PM 9 PM 10 PM 11 PM 12 AM	6 AM 7 AM 8 AM 9 AM 10 AM 11 AM 12 PM 1 PM 2 PM 3 PM 4 PM 5 PM 6 PM 7 PM 8 PM 9 PM 10 PM 11 PM 12 AM	6 AM 7 AM 8 AM 9 AM 10 AM 11 AM 12 PM 1 PM 2 PM 3 PM 4 PM 5 PM 6 PM 7 PM 8 PM 9 PM 10P M 11 PM 12 AM	6 AM 7 AM 8 AM 9 AM 10 AM 11 AM 12 PM 1 PM 2 PM 3 PM 4 PM 5 PM 6 PM 7 PM 8 PM 9 PM 10 PM 11 PM 12 AM
	MEAL	MEAL	MEAL	MEAL

S.L.E.E.P BEDTIME ROUTINE

ACTIVITIES FOR THE WEEK

FRIDAY

- ☐ WAKE (TIME)
- ☐ WORSHIP
- ☐ WORKOUT (TIME)
- ☐ WATER (#BOTTLES)

- ☐ SHOWER / BRUSH TEETH
- ☐ DRESS / HAIR CHECK
- ☐ MAKE BED / TIDY ROOM
- ☐ BREAKFAST

6 AM
7 AM
8 AM
9 AM
10 AM
11 AM
12 PM
1 PM
2 PM
3 PM
4 PM
5 PM
6 PM
7 PM
8 PM
9 PM
10 PM
11 PM
12 AM

SATURDAY

- ☐ WAKE (TIME)
- ☐ WORSHIP
- ☐ WORKOUT (TIME)
- ☐ WATER (#BOTTLES)

- ☐ SHOWER / BRUSH TEETH
- ☐ DRESS / HAIR CHECK
- ☐ MAKE BED / TIDY ROOM
- ☐ BREAKFAST

6 AM
7 AM
8 AM
9 AM
10 AM
11 AM
12 PM
1 PM
2 PM
3 PM
4 PM
5 PM
6 PM
7 PM
8 PM
9 PM
10 PM
11 PM
12 AM

SUNDAY

- ☐ WAKE (TIME)
- ☐ WORSHIP
- ☐ WORKOUT (TIME)
- ☐ WATER (#BOTTLES)

- ☐ SHOWER / BRUSH TEETH
- ☐ DRESS / HAIR CHECK
- ☐ MAKE BED / TIDY ROOM
- ☐ BREAKFAST

6 AM
7 AM
8 AM
9 AM
10 AM
11 AM
12 PM
1 PM
2 PM
3 PM
4 PM
5 PM
6 PM
7 PM
8 PM
9 PM
10 PM
11 PM
12 AM

PRAY & HUSTLE, HUSTLE & PRAY DAYTIME ROUTINE

REMINDERS / NOTES

MEAL

MEAL

MEAL

S.L.E.E.P BEDTIME ROUTINE

ACTIVITIES FOR THE WEEK

HAPPY THOUGHTS

	MONDAY	TUESDAY	WEDNESDAY	THURSDAY
4 W's WAKE ROUTINE	☐ WAKE (TIME)	☐ WAKE (TIME)	☐ WAKE (TIME)	☐ WAKE (TIME)
	☐ WORSHIP	☐ WORSHIP	☐ WORSHIP	☐ WORSHIP
	☐ WORKOUT (TIME)	☐ WORKOUT (TIME)	☐ WORKOUT (TIME)	☐ WORKOUT (TIME)
	☐ WATER (#BOTTLES)	☐ WATER (#BOTTLES)	☐ WATER (#BOTTLES)	☐ WATER (#BOTTLES)
SELF-CARE MORNING ROUTINE	☐ SHOWER / BRUSH TEETH	☐ SHOWER / BRUSH TEETH	☐ SHOWER / BRUSH TEETH	☐ SHOWER / BRUSH TEETH
	☐ DRESS / HAIR CHECK	☐ DRESS / HAIR CHECK	☐ DRESS / HAIR CHECK	☐ DRESS / HAIR CHECK
	☐ MAKE BED / TIDY ROOM	☐ MAKE BED / TIDY ROOM	☐ MAKE BED / TIDY ROOM	☐ MAKE BED / TIDY ROOM
	☐ BREAKFAST	☐ BREAKFAST	☐ BREAKFAST	☐ BREAKFAST
TIME	6 AM	6 AM	6 AM	6 AM
	7 AM	7 AM	7 AM	7 AM
	8 AM	8 AM	8 AM	8 AM
	9 AM	9 AM	9 AM	9 AM
	10 AM	10 AM	10 AM	10 AM
	11 AM	11 AM	11 AM	11 AM
	12 PM	12 PM	12 PM	12 PM
	1 PM	1 PM	1 PM	1 PM
	2 PM	2 PM	2 PM	2 PM
	3 PM	3 PM	3 PM	3 PM
	4 PM	4 PM	4 PM	4 PM
	5 PM	5 PM	5 PM	5 PM
	6 PM	6 PM	6 PM	6 PM
	7 PM	7 PM	7 PM	7 PM
	8 PM	8 PM	8 PM	8 PM
	9 PM	9 PM	9 PM	9 PM
	10 PM	10 PM	10P M	10 PM
	11 PM	11 PM	11 PM	11 PM
	12 AM	12 AM	12 AM	12 AM
	MEAL	**MEAL**	**MEAL**	**MEAL**

S.L.E.E.P BEDTIME ROUTINE

ACTIVITIES FOR THE WEEK

FRIDAY

☐ WAKE (TIME) _____
☐ WORSHIP _____
☐ WORKOUT (TIME) _____
☐ WATER (#BOTTLES) _____

☐ SHOWER / BRUSH TEETH
☐ DRESS / HAIR CHECK
☐ MAKE BED / TIDY ROOM
☐ BREAKFAST

6 AM
7 AM
8 AM
9 AM
10 AM
11 AM
12 PM
1 PM
2 PM
3 PM
4 PM
5 PM
6 PM
7 PM
8 PM
9 PM
10 PM
11 PM
12 AM

SATURDAY

☐ WAKE (TIME) _____
☐ WORSHIP _____
☐ WORKOUT (TIME) _____
☐ WATER (#BOTTLES) _____

☐ SHOWER / BRUSH TEETH
☐ DRESS / HAIR CHECK
☐ MAKE BED / TIDY ROOM
☐ BREAKFAST

6 AM
7 AM
8 AM
9 AM
10 AM
11 AM
12 PM
1 PM
2 PM
3 PM
4 PM
5 PM
6 PM
7 PM
8 PM
9 PM
10 PM
11 PM
12 AM

SUNDAY

☐ WAKE (TIME) _____
☐ WORSHIP _____
☐ WORKOUT (TIME) _____
☐ WATER (#BOTTLES) _____

☐ SHOWER / BRUSH TEETH
☐ DRESS / HAIR CHECK
☐ MAKE BED / TIDY ROOM
☐ BREAKFAST

6 AM
7 AM
8 AM
9 AM
10 AM
11 AM
12 PM
1 PM
2 PM
3 PM
4 PM
5 PM
6 PM
7 PM
8 PM
9 PM
10 PM
11 PM
12 AM

PRAY & HUSTLE, HUSTLE & PRAY DAYTIME ROUTINE

REMINDERS / NOTES

MEAL

MEAL

MEAL

S.L.E.E.P BEDTIME ROUTINE

ACTIVITIES FOR THE WEEK

HAPPY THOUGHTS

MONTH _____

	MONDAY	TUESDAY	WEDNESDAY	THURSDAY
4 W's WAKE ROUTINE	☐ WAKE (TIME) ☐ WORSHIP ☐ WORKOUT (TIME) ☐ WATER (#BOTTLES)	☐ WAKE (TIME) ☐ WORSHIP ☐ WORKOUT (TIME) ☐ WATER (#BOTTLES)	☐ WAKE (TIME) ☐ WORSHIP ☐ WORKOUT (TIME) ☐ WATER (#BOTTLES)	☐ WAKE (TIME) ☐ WORSHIP ☐ WORKOUT (TIME) ☐ WATER (#BOTTLES)
SELF-CARE MORNING ROUTINE	☐ SHOWER / BRUSH TEETH ☐ DRESS / HAIR CHECK ☐ MAKE BED / TIDY ROOM ☐ BREAKFAST	☐ SHOWER / BRUSH TEETH ☐ DRESS / HAIR CHECK ☐ MAKE BED / TIDY ROOM ☐ BREAKFAST	☐ SHOWER / BRUSH TEETH ☐ DRESS / HAIR CHECK ☐ MAKE BED / TIDY ROOM ☐ BREAKFAST	☐ SHOWER / BRUSH TEETH ☐ DRESS / HAIR CHECK ☐ MAKE BED / TIDY ROOM ☐ BREAKFAST
TIME	6 AM 7 AM 8 AM 9 AM 10 AM 11 AM 12 PM 1 PM 2 PM 3 PM 4 PM 5 PM 6 PM 7 PM 8 PM 9 PM 10 PM 11 PM 12 AM	6 AM 7 AM 8 AM 9 AM 10 AM 11 AM 12 PM 1 PM 2 PM 3 PM 4 PM 5 PM 6 PM 7 PM 8 PM 9 PM 10 PM 11 PM 12 AM	6 AM 7 AM 8 AM 9 AM 10 AM 11 AM 12 PM 1 PM 2 PM 3 PM 4 PM 5 PM 6 PM 7 PM 8 PM 9 PM 10P M 11 PM 12 AM	6 AM 7 AM 8 AM 9 AM 10 AM 11 AM 12 PM 1 PM 2 PM 3 PM 4 PM 5 PM 6 PM 7 PM 8 PM 9 PM 10 PM 11 PM 12 AM
	MEAL	MEAL	MEAL	MEAL

S.L.E.E.P BEDTIME ROUTINE

ACTIVITIES FOR THE WEEK

BIBLE VERSE OF THE WEEK _____

FRIDAY	SATURDAY	SUNDAY
☐ WAKE (TIME)	☐ WAKE (TIME)	☐ WAKE (TIME)
☐ WORSHIP	☐ WORSHIP	☐ WORSHIP
☐ WORKOUT (TIME)	☐ WORKOUT (TIME)	☐ WORKOUT (TIME)
☐ WATER (#BOTTLES)	☐ WATER (#BOTTLES)	☐ WATER (#BOTTLES)
☐ SHOWER / BRUSH TEETH	☐ SHOWER / BRUSH TEETH	☐ SHOWER / BRUSH TEETH
☐ DRESS / HAIR CHECK	☐ DRESS / HAIR CHECK	☐ DRESS / HAIR CHECK
☐ MAKE BED / TIDY ROOM	☐ MAKE BED / TIDY ROOM	☐ MAKE BED / TIDY ROOM
☐ BREAKFAST	☐ BREAKFAST	☐ BREAKFAST

PRAY & HUSTLE, HUSTLE & PRAY DAYTIME ROUTINE

FRIDAY	SATURDAY	SUNDAY
6 AM	6 AM	6 AM
7 AM	7 AM	7 AM
8 AM	8 AM	8 AM
9 AM	9 AM	9 AM
10 AM	10 AM	10 AM
11 AM	11 AM	11 AM
12 PM	12 PM	12 PM
1 PM	1 PM	1 PM
2 PM	2 PM	2 PM
3 PM	3 PM	3 PM
4 PM	4 PM	4 PM
5 PM	5 PM	5 PM
6 PM	6 PM	6 PM
7 PM	7 PM	7 PM
8 PM	8 PM	8 PM
9 PM	9 PM	9 PM
10 PM	10 PM	10 PM
11 PM	11 PM	11 PM
12 AM	12 AM	12 AM

REMINDERS / NOTES

MEAL	MEAL	MEAL

S.L.E.E.P BEDTIME ROUTINE

ACTIVITIES FOR THE WEEK

HAPPY THOUGHTS

MONTH _____

	MONDAY	TUESDAY	WEDNESDAY	THURSDAY
4 W's WAKE ROUTINE	☐ WAKE (TIME) ☐ WORSHIP ☐ WORKOUT (TIME) ☐ WATER (#BOTTLES)	☐ WAKE (TIME) ☐ WORSHIP ☐ WORKOUT (TIME) ☐ WATER (#BOTTLES)	☐ WAKE (TIME) ☐ WORSHIP ☐ WORKOUT (TIME) ☐ WATER (#BOTTLES)	☐ WAKE (TIME) ☐ WORSHIP ☐ WORKOUT (TIME) ☐ WATER (#BOTTLES)
SELF-CARE MORNING ROUTINE	☐ SHOWER / BRUSH TEETH ☐ DRESS / HAIR CHECK ☐ MAKE BED / TIDY ROOM ☐ BREAKFAST	☐ SHOWER / BRUSH TEETH ☐ DRESS / HAIR CHECK ☐ MAKE BED / TIDY ROOM ☐ BREAKFAST	☐ SHOWER / BRUSH TEETH ☐ DRESS / HAIR CHECK ☐ MAKE BED / TIDY ROOM ☐ BREAKFAST	☐ SHOWER / BRUSH TEETH ☐ DRESS / HAIR CHECK ☐ MAKE BED / TIDY ROOM ☐ BREAKFAST
TIME	6 AM 7 AM 8 AM 9 AM 10 AM 11 AM 12 PM 1 PM 2 PM 3 PM 4 PM 5 PM 6 PM 7 PM 8 PM 9 PM 10 PM 11 PM 12 AM	6 AM 7 AM 8 AM 9 AM 10 AM 11 AM 12 PM 1 PM 2 PM 3 PM 4 PM 5 PM 6 PM 7 PM 8 PM 9 PM 10 PM 11 PM 12 AM	6 AM 7 AM 8 AM 9 AM 10 AM 11 AM 12 PM 1 PM 2 PM 3 PM 4 PM 5 PM 6 PM 7 PM 8 PM 9 PM 10P M 11 PM 12 AM	6 AM 7 AM 8 AM 9 AM 10 AM 11 AM 12 PM 1 PM 2 PM 3 PM 4 PM 5 PM 6 PM 7 PM 8 PM 9 PM 10 PM 11 PM 12 AM
	MEAL	MEAL	MEAL	MEAL

S.L.E.E.P BEDTIME ROUTINE

ACTIVITIES FOR THE WEEK

BIBLE VERSE OF THE WEEK _____

FRIDAY	SATURDAY	SUNDAY
□ WAKE (TIME)	□ WAKE (TIME)	□ WAKE (TIME)
□ WORSHIP	□ WORSHIP	□ WORSHIP
□ WORKOUT (TIME)	□ WORKOUT (TIME)	□ WORKOUT (TIME)
□ WATER (#BOTTLES)	□ WATER (#BOTTLES)	□ WATER (#BOTTLES)
□ SHOWER / BRUSH TEETH	□ SHOWER / BRUSH TEETH	□ SHOWER / BRUSH TEETH
□ DRESS / HAIR CHECK	□ DRESS / HAIR CHECK	□ DRESS / HAIR CHECK
□ MAKE BED / TIDY ROOM	□ MAKE BED / TIDY ROOM	□ MAKE BED / TIDY ROOM
□ BREAKFAST	□ BREAKFAST	□ BREAKFAST

PRAY & HUSTLE, HUSTLE & PRAY DAYTIME ROUTINE

_____
_____
_____
_____

FRIDAY	SATURDAY	SUNDAY
6 AM	6 AM	6 AM
7 AM	7 AM	7 AM
8 AM	8 AM	8 AM
9 AM	9 AM	9 AM
10 AM	10 AM	10 AM
11 AM	11 AM	11 AM
12 PM	12 PM	12 PM
1 PM	1 PM	1 PM
2 PM	2 PM	2 PM
3 PM	3 PM	3 PM
4 PM	4 PM	4 PM
5 PM	5 PM	5 PM
6 PM	6 PM	6 PM
7 PM	7 PM	7 PM
8 PM	8 PM	8 PM
9 PM	9 PM	9 PM
10 PM	10 PM	10 PM
11 PM	11 PM	11 PM
12 AM	12 AM	12 AM

REMINDERS / NOTES

_____
_____
_____
_____
_____

MEAL	MEAL	MEAL

S.L.E.E.P BEDTIME ROUTINE

HAPPY THOUGHTS
_____
_____
_____
_____
_____

ACTIVITIES FOR THE WEEK

MONTH _____

	MONDAY	**TUESDAY**	**WEDNESDAY**	**THURSDAY**
4 W's WAKE ROUTINE	□ WAKE (TIME) ___ □ WORSHIP ___ □ WORKOUT (TIME) ___ □ WATER (#BOTTLES) ___	□ WAKE (TIME) ___ □ WORSHIP ___ □ WORKOUT (TIME) ___ □ WATER (#BOTTLES) ___	□ WAKE (TIME) ___ □ WORSHIP ___ □ WORKOUT (TIME) ___ □ WATER (#BOTTLES) ___	□ WAKE (TIME) ___ □ WORSHIP ___ □ WORKOUT (TIME) ___ □ WATER (#BOTTLES) ___
SELF-CARE MORNING ROUTINE	□ SHOWER / BRUSH TEETH □ DRESS / HAIR CHECK □ MAKE BED / TIDY ROOM □ BREAKFAST	□ SHOWER / BRUSH TEETH □ DRESS / HAIR CHECK □ MAKE BED / TIDY ROOM □ BREAKFAST	□ SHOWER / BRUSH TEETH □ DRESS / HAIR CHECK □ MAKE BED / TIDY ROOM □ BREAKFAST	□ SHOWER / BRUSH TEETH □ DRESS / HAIR CHECK □ MAKE BED / TIDY ROOM □ BREAKFAST
TIME	6 AM 7 AM 8 AM 9 AM 10 AM 11 AM 12 PM 1 PM 2 PM 3 PM 4 PM 5 PM 6 PM 7 PM 8 PM 9 PM 10 PM 11 PM 12 AM	6 AM 7 AM 8 AM 9 AM 10 AM 11 AM 12 PM 1 PM 2 PM 3 PM 4 PM 5 PM 6 PM 7 PM 8 PM 9 PM 10 PM 11 PM 12 AM	6 AM 7 AM 8 AM 9 AM 10 AM 11 AM 12 PM 1 PM 2 PM 3 PM 4 PM 5 PM 6 PM 7 PM 8 PM 9 PM 10P M 11 PM 12 AM	6 AM 7 AM 8 AM 9 AM 10 AM 11 AM 12 PM 1 PM 2 PM 3 PM 4 PM 5 PM 6 PM 7 PM 8 PM 9 PM 10 PM 11 PM 12 AM
	MEAL	**MEAL**	**MEAL**	**MEAL**

S.L.E.E.P BEDTIME ROUTINE

ACTIVITIES FOR THE WEEK

BIBLE VERSE OF THE WEEK _____

FRIDAY	SATURDAY	SUNDAY
☐ WAKE (TIME)	☐ WAKE (TIME)	☐ WAKE (TIME)
☐ WORSHIP	☐ WORSHIP	☐ WORSHIP
☐ WORKOUT (TIME)	☐ WORKOUT (TIME)	☐ WORKOUT (TIME)
☐ WATER (#BOTTLES)	☐ WATER (#BOTTLES)	☐ WATER (#BOTTLES)
☐ SHOWER / BRUSH TEETH	☐ SHOWER / BRUSH TEETH	☐ SHOWER / BRUSH TEETH
☐ DRESS / HAIR CHECK	☐ DRESS / HAIR CHECK	☐ DRESS / HAIR CHECK
☐ MAKE BED / TIDY ROOM	☐ MAKE BED / TIDY ROOM	☐ MAKE BED / TIDY ROOM
☐ BREAKFAST	☐ BREAKFAST	☐ BREAKFAST

PRAY & HUSTLE, HUSTLE & PRAY DAYTIME ROUTINE

FRIDAY	SATURDAY	SUNDAY
6 AM	6 AM	6 AM
7 AM	7 AM	7 AM
8 AM	8 AM	8 AM
9 AM	9 AM	9 AM
10 AM	10 AM	10 AM
11 AM	11 AM	11 AM
12 PM	12 PM	12 PM
1 PM	1 PM	1 PM
2 PM	2 PM	2 PM
3 PM	3 PM	3 PM
4 PM	4 PM	4 PM
5 PM	5 PM	5 PM
6 PM	6 PM	6 PM
7 PM	7 PM	7 PM
8 PM	8 PM	8 PM
9 PM	9 PM	9 PM
10 PM	10 PM	10 PM
11 PM	11 PM	11 PM
12 AM	12 AM	12 AM

REMINDERS / NOTES

MEAL   MEAL   MEAL

S.L.E.E.P BEDTIME ROUTINE

HAPPY THOUGHTS

ACTIVITIES FOR THE WEEK

	MONDAY	TUESDAY	WEDNESDAY	THURSDAY
4 W's WAKE ROUTINE	☐ WAKE (TIME) ☐ WORSHIP ☐ WORKOUT (TIME) ☐ WATER (#BOTTLES)	☐ WAKE (TIME) ☐ WORSHIP ☐ WORKOUT (TIME) ☐ WATER (#BOTTLES)	☐ WAKE (TIME) ☐ WORSHIP ☐ WORKOUT (TIME) ☐ WATER (#BOTTLES)	☐ WAKE (TIME) ☐ WORSHIP ☐ WORKOUT (TIME) ☐ WATER (#BOTTLES)
SELF-CARE MORNING ROUTINE	☐ SHOWER / BRUSH TEETH ☐ DRESS / HAIR CHECK ☐ MAKE BED / TIDY ROOM ☐ BREAKFAST	☐ SHOWER / BRUSH TEETH ☐ DRESS / HAIR CHECK ☐ MAKE BED / TIDY ROOM ☐ BREAKFAST	☐ SHOWER / BRUSH TEETH ☐ DRESS / HAIR CHECK ☐ MAKE BED / TIDY ROOM ☐ BREAKFAST	☐ SHOWER / BRUSH TEETH ☐ DRESS / HAIR CHECK ☐ MAKE BED / TIDY ROOM ☐ BREAKFAST
TIME	6 AM 7 AM 8 AM 9 AM 10 AM 11 AM 12 PM 1 PM 2 PM 3 PM 4 PM 5 PM 6 PM 7 PM 8 PM 9 PM 10 PM 11 PM 12 AM	6 AM 7 AM 8 AM 9 AM 10 AM 11 AM 12 PM 1 PM 2 PM 3 PM 4 PM 5 PM 6 PM 7 PM 8 PM 9 PM 10 PM 11 PM 12 AM	6 AM 7 AM 8 AM 9 AM 10 AM 11 AM 12 PM 1 PM 2 PM 3 PM 4 PM 5 PM 6 PM 7 PM 8 PM 9 PM 10P M 11 PM 12 AM	6 AM 7 AM 8 AM 9 AM 10 AM 11 AM 12 PM 1 PM 2 PM 3 PM 4 PM 5 PM 6 PM 7 PM 8 PM 9 PM 10 PM 11 PM 12 AM
	MEAL	MEAL	MEAL	MEAL
	_____	_____	_____	_____

S.L.E.E.P BEDTIME ROUTINE

_____   _____   _____   _____

_____   _____   _____   _____

ACTIVITIES FOR THE WEEK

_____   _____   _____   _____

FRIDAY

- ☐ WAKE (TIME) _____
- ☐ WORSHIP _____
- ☐ WORKOUT (TIME) _____
- ☐ WATER (#BOTTLES) _____

- ☐ SHOWER / BRUSH TEETH
- ☐ DRESS / HAIR CHECK
- ☐ MAKE BED / TIDY ROOM
- ☐ BREAKFAST

6 AM _____
7 AM _____
8 AM _____
9 AM _____
10 AM _____
11 AM _____
12 PM _____
1 PM _____
2 PM _____
3 PM _____
4 PM _____
5 PM _____
6 PM _____
7 PM _____
8 PM _____
9 PM _____
10 PM _____
11 PM _____
12 AM _____

SATURDAY

- ☐ WAKE (TIME) _____
- ☐ WORSHIP _____
- ☐ WORKOUT (TIME) _____
- ☐ WATER (#BOTTLES) _____

- ☐ SHOWER / BRUSH TEETH
- ☐ DRESS / HAIR CHECK
- ☐ MAKE BED / TIDY ROOM
- ☐ BREAKFAST

6 AM _____
7 AM _____
8 AM _____
9 AM _____
10 AM _____
11 AM _____
12 PM _____
1 PM _____
2 PM _____
3 PM _____
4 PM _____
5 PM _____
6 PM _____
7 PM _____
8 PM _____
9 PM _____
10 PM _____
11 PM _____
12 AM _____

SUNDAY

- ☐ WAKE (TIME) _____
- ☐ WORSHIP _____
- ☐ WORKOUT (TIME) _____
- ☐ WATER (#BOTTLES) _____

- ☐ SHOWER / BRUSH TEETH
- ☐ DRESS / HAIR CHECK
- ☐ MAKE BED / TIDY ROOM
- ☐ BREAKFAST

6 AM _____
7 AM _____
8 AM _____
9 AM _____
10 AM _____
11 AM _____
12 PM _____
1 PM _____
2 PM _____
3 PM _____
4 PM _____
5 PM _____
6 PM _____
7 PM _____
8 PM _____
9 PM _____
10 PM _____
11 PM _____
12 AM _____

PRAY & HUSTLE, HUSTLE & PRAY DAYTIME ROUTINE

_____
_____
_____
_____
_____

REMINDERS / NOTES

_____
_____
_____
_____
_____
_____
_____
_____

MEAL _____

MEAL _____

MEAL _____

S.L.E.E.P BEDTIME ROUTINE

HAPPY THOUGHTS

_____
_____
_____
_____
_____

ACTIVITIES FOR THE WEEK

_____   _____   _____

	MONDAY	TUESDAY	WEDNESDAY	THURSDAY
4 W's WAKE ROUTINE	☐ WAKE (TIME) _____ ☐ WORSHIP ☐ WORKOUT (TIME) _____ ☐ WATER (#BOTTLES)	☐ WAKE (TIME) _____ ☐ WORSHIP ☐ WORKOUT (TIME) _____ ☐ WATER (#BOTTLES)	☐ WAKE (TIME) _____ ☐ WORSHIP ☐ WORKOUT (TIME) _____ ☐ WATER (#BOTTLES)	☐ WAKE (TIME) _____ ☐ WORSHIP ☐ WORKOUT (TIME) _____ ☐ WATER (#BOTTLES)
SELF-CARE MORNING ROUTINE	☐ SHOWER / BRUSH TEETH ☐ DRESS / HAIR CHECK ☐ MAKE BED / TIDY ROOM ☐ BREAKFAST	☐ SHOWER / BRUSH TEETH ☐ DRESS / HAIR CHECK ☐ MAKE BED / TIDY ROOM ☐ BREAKFAST	☐ SHOWER / BRUSH TEETH ☐ DRESS / HAIR CHECK ☐ MAKE BED / TIDY ROOM ☐ BREAKFAST	☐ SHOWER / BRUSH TEETH ☐ DRESS / HAIR CHECK ☐ MAKE BED / TIDY ROOM ☐ BREAKFAST
TIME	6 AM 7 AM 8 AM 9 AM 10 AM 11 AM 12 PM 1 PM 2 PM 3 PM 4 PM 5 PM 6 PM 7 PM 8 PM 9 PM 10 PM 11 PM 12 AM	6 AM 7 AM 8 AM 9 AM 10 AM 11 AM 12 PM 1 PM 2 PM 3 PM 4 PM 5 PM 6 PM 7 PM 8 PM 9 PM 10 PM 11 PM 12 AM	6 AM 7 AM 8 AM 9 AM 10 AM 11 AM 12 PM 1 PM 2 PM 3 PM 4 PM 5 PM 6 PM 7 PM 8 PM 9 PM 10P M 11 PM 12 AM	6 AM 7 AM 8 AM 9 AM 10 AM 11 AM 12 PM 1 PM 2 PM 3 PM 4 PM 5 PM 6 PM 7 PM 8 PM 9 PM 10 PM 11 PM 12 AM
MEAL				

S.L.E.E.P BEDTIME ROUTINE

ACTIVITIES FOR THE WEEK

BIBLE VERSE OF THE WEEK _____

FRIDAY	SATURDAY	SUNDAY
□ WAKE (TIME)	□ WAKE (TIME)	□ WAKE (TIME)
□ WORSHIP	□ WORSHIP	□ WORSHIP
□ WORKOUT (TIME)	□ WORKOUT (TIME)	□ WORKOUT (TIME)
□ WATER (#BOTTLES)	□ WATER (#BOTTLES)	□ WATER (#BOTTLES)
□ SHOWER / BRUSH TEETH	□ SHOWER / BRUSH TEETH	□ SHOWER / BRUSH TEETH
□ DRESS / HAIR CHECK	□ DRESS / HAIR CHECK	□ DRESS / HAIR CHECK
□ MAKE BED / TIDY ROOM	□ MAKE BED / TIDY ROOM	□ MAKE BED / TIDY ROOM
□ BREAKFAST	□ BREAKFAST	□ BREAKFAST

PRAY & HUSTLE, HUSTLE & PRAY DAYTIME ROUTINE

FRIDAY	SATURDAY	SUNDAY
6 AM	6 AM	6 AM
7 AM	7 AM	7 AM
8 AM	8 AM	8 AM
9 AM	9 AM	9 AM
10 AM	10 AM	10 AM
11 AM	11 AM	11 AM
12 PM	12 PM	12 PM
1 PM	1 PM	1 PM
2 PM	2 PM	2 PM
3 PM	3 PM	3 PM
4 PM	4 PM	4 PM
5 PM	5 PM	5 PM
6 PM	6 PM	6 PM
7 PM	7 PM	7 PM
8 PM	8 PM	8 PM
9 PM	9 PM	9 PM
10 PM	10 PM	10 PM
11 PM	11 PM	11 PM
12 AM	12 AM	12 AM

REMINDERS / NOTES

MEAL	MEAL	MEAL

S.L.E.E.P BEDTIME ROUTINE

HAPPY THOUGHTS

ACTIVITIES FOR THE WEEK

	MONDAY	TUESDAY	WEDNESDAY	THURSDAY
4 W's WAKE ROUTINE	☐ WAKE (TIME) ☐ WORSHIP ☐ WORKOUT (TIME) ☐ WATER (#BOTTLES)	☐ WAKE (TIME) ☐ WORSHIP ☐ WORKOUT (TIME) ☐ WATER (#BOTTLES)	☐ WAKE (TIME) ☐ WORSHIP ☐ WORKOUT (TIME) ☐ WATER (#BOTTLES)	☐ WAKE (TIME) ☐ WORSHIP ☐ WORKOUT (TIME) ☐ WATER (#BOTTLES)
SELF-CARE MORNING ROUTINE	☐ SHOWER / BRUSH TEETH ☐ DRESS / HAIR CHECK ☐ MAKE BED / TIDY ROOM ☐ BREAKFAST	☐ SHOWER / BRUSH TEETH ☐ DRESS / HAIR CHECK ☐ MAKE BED / TIDY ROOM ☐ BREAKFAST	☐ SHOWER / BRUSH TEETH ☐ DRESS / HAIR CHECK ☐ MAKE BED / TIDY ROOM ☐ BREAKFAST	☐ SHOWER / BRUSH TEETH ☐ DRESS / HAIR CHECK ☐ MAKE BED / TIDY ROOM ☐ BREAKFAST
TIME	6 AM 7 AM 8 AM 9 AM 10 AM 11 AM 12 PM 1 PM 2 PM 3 PM 4 PM 5 PM 6 PM 7 PM 8 PM 9 PM 10 PM 11 PM 12 AM	6 AM 7 AM 8 AM 9 AM 10 AM 11 AM 12 PM 1 PM 2 PM 3 PM 4 PM 5 PM 6 PM 7 PM 8 PM 9 PM 10 PM 11 PM 12 AM	6 AM 7 AM 8 AM 9 AM 10 AM 11 AM 12 PM 1 PM 2 PM 3 PM 4 PM 5 PM 6 PM 7 PM 8 PM 9 PM 10P M 11 PM 12 AM	6 AM 7 AM 8 AM 9 AM 10 AM 11 AM 12 PM 1 PM 2 PM 3 PM 4 PM 5 PM 6 PM 7 PM 8 PM 9 PM 10 PM 11 PM 12 AM

MEAL	MEAL	MEAL	MEAL
_____	_____	_____	_____

S.L.E.E.P BEDTIME ROUTINE

ACTIVITIES FOR THE WEEK

BIBLE VERSE OF THE WEEK _____

FRIDAY	SATURDAY	SUNDAY
☐ WAKE (TIME)	☐ WAKE (TIME)	☐ WAKE (TIME)
☐ WORSHIP	☐ WORSHIP	☐ WORSHIP
☐ WORKOUT (TIME)	☐ WORKOUT (TIME)	☐ WORKOUT (TIME)
☐ WATER (#BOTTLES)	☐ WATER (#BOTTLES)	☐ WATER (#BOTTLES)
☐ SHOWER / BRUSH TEETH	☐ SHOWER / BRUSH TEETH	☐ SHOWER / BRUSH TEETH
☐ DRESS / HAIR CHECK	☐ DRESS / HAIR CHECK	☐ DRESS / HAIR CHECK
☐ MAKE BED / TIDY ROOM	☐ MAKE BED / TIDY ROOM	☐ MAKE BED / TIDY ROOM
☐ BREAKFAST	☐ BREAKFAST	☐ BREAKFAST

PRAY & HUSTLE, HUSTLE & PRAY DAYTIME ROUTINE

FRIDAY	SATURDAY	SUNDAY
6 AM	6 AM	6 AM
7 AM	7 AM	7 AM
8 AM	8 AM	8 AM
9 AM	9 AM	9 AM
10 AM	10 AM	10 AM
11 AM	11 AM	11 AM
12 PM	12 PM	12 PM
1 PM	1 PM	1 PM
2 PM	2 PM	2 PM
3 PM	3 PM	3 PM
4 PM	4 PM	4 PM
5 PM	5 PM	5 PM
6 PM	6 PM	6 PM
7 PM	7 PM	7 PM
8 PM	8 PM	8 PM
9 PM	9 PM	9 PM
10 PM	10 PM	10 PM
11 PM	11 PM	11 PM
12 AM	12 AM	12 AM

REMINDERS / NOTES

MEAL	MEAL	MEAL

S.L.E.E.P BEDTIME ROUTINE

ACTIVITIES FOR THE WEEK

HAPPY THOUGHTS

131

MONTH _____

	MONDAY	TUESDAY	WEDNESDAY	THURSDAY
4 W's WAKE ROUTINE	□ WAKE (TIME) □ WORSHIP □ WORKOUT (TIME) □ WATER (#BOTTLES)	□ WAKE (TIME) □ WORSHIP □ WORKOUT (TIME) □ WATER (#BOTTLES)	□ WAKE (TIME) □ WORSHIP □ WORKOUT (TIME) □ WATER (#BOTTLES)	□ WAKE (TIME) □ WORSHIP □ WORKOUT (TIME) □ WATER (#BOTTLES)
SELF-CARE MORNING ROUTINE	□ SHOWER / BRUSH TEETH □ DRESS / HAIR CHECK □ MAKE BED / TIDY ROOM □ BREAKFAST	□ SHOWER / BRUSH TEETH □ DRESS / HAIR CHECK □ MAKE BED / TIDY ROOM □ BREAKFAST	□ SHOWER / BRUSH TEETH □ DRESS / HAIR CHECK □ MAKE BED / TIDY ROOM □ BREAKFAST	□ SHOWER / BRUSH TEETH □ DRESS / HAIR CHECK □ MAKE BED / TIDY ROOM □ BREAKFAST
TIME	6 AM 7 AM 8 AM 9 AM 10 AM 11 AM 12 PM 1 PM 2 PM 3 PM 4 PM 5 PM 6 PM 7 PM 8 PM 9 PM 10 PM 11 PM 12 AM	6 AM 7 AM 8 AM 9 AM 10 AM 11 AM 12 PM 1 PM 2 PM 3 PM 4 PM 5 PM 6 PM 7 PM 8 PM 9 PM 10 PM 11 PM 12 AM	6 AM 7 AM 8 AM 9 AM 10 AM 11 AM 12 PM 1 PM 2 PM 3 PM 4 PM 5 PM 6 PM 7 PM 8 PM 9 PM 10P M 11 PM 12 AM	6 AM 7 AM 8 AM 9 AM 10 AM 11 AM 12 PM 1 PM 2 PM 3 PM 4 PM 5 PM 6 PM 7 PM 8 PM 9 PM 10 PM 11 PM 12 AM
	MEAL	**MEAL**	**MEAL**	**MEAL**

S.L.E.E.P BEDTIME ROUTINE

_____

ACTIVITIES FOR THE WEEK

_____

FRIDAY	SATURDAY	SUNDAY

PRAY & HUSTLE, HUSTLE & PRAY DAYTIME ROUTINE

☐ WAKE (TIME)	☐ WAKE (TIME)	☐ WAKE (TIME)
☐ WORSHIP	☐ WORSHIP	☐ WORSHIP
☐ WORKOUT (TIME)	☐ WORKOUT (TIME)	☐ WORKOUT (TIME)
☐ WATER (#BOTTLES)	☐ WATER (#BOTTLES)	☐ WATER (#BOTTLES)
☐ SHOWER / BRUSH TEETH	☐ SHOWER / BRUSH TEETH	☐ SHOWER / BRUSH TEETH
☐ DRESS / HAIR CHECK	☐ DRESS / HAIR CHECK	☐ DRESS / HAIR CHECK
☐ MAKE BED / TIDY ROOM	☐ MAKE BED / TIDY ROOM	☐ MAKE BED / TIDY ROOM
☐ BREAKFAST	☐ BREAKFAST	☐ BREAKFAST

FRIDAY	SATURDAY	SUNDAY
6 AM	6 AM	6 AM
7 AM	7 AM	7 AM
8 AM	8 AM	8 AM
9 AM	9 AM	9 AM
10 AM	10 AM	10 AM
11 AM	11 AM	11 AM
12 PM	12 PM	12 PM
1 PM	1 PM	1 PM
2 PM	2 PM	2 PM
3 PM	3 PM	3 PM
4 PM	4 PM	4 PM
5 PM	5 PM	5 PM
6 PM	6 PM	6 PM
7 PM	7 PM	7 PM
8 PM	8 PM	8 PM
9 PM	9 PM	9 PM
10 PM	10 PM	10 PM
11 PM	11 PM	11 PM
12 AM	12 AM	12 AM

REMINDERS / NOTES

MEAL	MEAL	MEAL

S.L.E.E.P BEDTIME ROUTINE

HAPPY THOUGHTS

ACTIVITIES FOR THE WEEK

FAMILY MEDICATION TRACKER

DATE / TIME	MEDICATION	DOSAGE / AMOUNT	GIVEN TO	PHYSICIAN

ROYAL EAGLE MOM

WEEKLY HOUSE CLEANING SCHEDULE

As mothers, part of our duty and responsibility is to maintain a happy, healthy, clean, and comfortable living environment for our family, even if this means delegating chores and tackling one area at a time. Provided is a sample schedule that breaks down areas that can be tackled each day, week, and month. The areas of the home can be deep cleaned or tidied up. You will be surprised that sticking to a schedule can maintain good cleaning habits. A tidy home has been shown to have some positive effect on mental status and well-being, while a cluttered home can have a negative effect.

The purpose of the weekly cleaning sample schedule and template is to help cultivate a healthy home environment.

MONDAY	**KITCHEN**	☐ Clean sink and counters ☐ Straighten cabinets and drawers ☐ Wipe all appliances ☐ Wipe cabinets and walls ☐ Sweep and mop
TUESDAY	**LIVING ROOM**	☐ Vacuum, sweep and mop ☐ Organize toys and shelves ☐ Dust, polish and windows ☐ Clean under the couch
WEDNESDAY	**BEDROOMS**	☐ Straighten closet and drawers ☐ Dust curtains, windows, furniture and mirrors ☐ Vacuum, sweep and mop
THURSDAY	**BATHROOMS**	☐ Clean shower, toilet and sinks ☐ Scrub counters and mirrors ☐ Wash rugs (include kitchen) ☐ Sweep and mop
FRIDAY	**ENTRY & HALLS**	☐ De-clutter and organize ☐ Sweep and mop ☐ Clean mirror ☐ Spot clean bench
WEEKEND	**CLEAN-UP**	☐ Meal plan ☐ Groceries ☐ What's left over from the week?

EVERYDAY

☐ Make bed
☐ Dishes
☐ Pick-up toys and all miscellaneous
☐ Wipe counters

☐ 1 Load Laundry
☐ Put away clothes
☐ Take out trash
☐ Water plants

BI-WEEKLY

☐ Change sheets
☐ Wash couch blankets and pillows
☐ Dust curtains and baseboards

☐ Clean out fridge
☐ Wash towels
☐ Clean backyard

MONTHLY

☐ Straighten closet and drawers
☐ Dust curtains, windows, furniture and mirrors

☐ Vacuum, sweep and mop
☐ Trim grass

MONDAY	KITCHEN	☐☐☐☐☐☐☐☐
TUESDAY	LIVING ROOM	☐☐☐☐☐☐☐
WEDNESDAY	BEDROOMS	☐☐☐☐☐☐
THURSDAY	BATHROOMS	☐☐☐☐☐☐☐☐
FRIDAY	ENTRY AND HALLS	☐☐☐☐☐☐☐
WEEKEND	CLEAN-UP	☐☐☐☐☐☐
EVERYDAY	☐☐☐☐	☐☐☐☐
BI-WEEKLY	☐☐☐☐	☐☐☐☐
MONTHLY	☐☐☐☐	☐☐☐☐

INSPIRATIONAL BIBLE
VERSES & DEVOTIONS

Here is a list of suggested devotional scriptures. The following scriptures can be used as daily devotions or affirmations. The verses are listed as inspirational and encouraging words to stay strong, to live life in love, and to be strong in our roles. Reference and open your Bible to these verses. Meditate on the verses as they become part of your Royal Eagle lifestyle.

Suggested Scriptures

Deuteronomy 6:4-9   "The Shema Prayer"

These few verses lay a foundation of faith and love. In the Jewish culture, mothers lay the foundation of love and faith in God, parents, family, and mankind. It builds a strong source of faith in God, our Creator. The scriptures are taught as a prayer that the children say twice a day. This encourages a prayer lifestyle, which is an important part of being an Eagle Mom!

John 3:16   "Unconditional Love"

Love conquers all. As an Eagle Moms, we must cultivate the mentality of doing everything in love. Children may test our patience. We may yell or have a "mommy tantrum," but love must triumph over any issues. We must always remember to raise our children in love. Choose love over rules or discipline.

Psalm 51:10   "A Clean Heart"

This verse reminds us to keep personal values and to raise our children with sound values. As an Eagle Moms, we must be humble and have a clean heart. Be honest and find delightful freedom in truth.

Matthew 6:9–13   "The Lord's Prayer"

As an Eagle Moms, we must lead by example. Eagle Moms cultivate a lifestyle of prayer; therefore, we will encourage our children to do the same. Teach your children to pray and live a prayer lifestyle by guiding them in the Lord's Prayer. Encourage your children to pray in their secret place and from their hearts. Encourage them to pray during adversity. Encourage them to pray and give thanks even when life is going well. *(Remember P.R.A.Y.: Praise and thank God / Repent / Ask God for your desires and needs / Yield and wait for his direction.)*

Philippians 4:13   "Confidence"

Living in love and showing love builds confidence. Use this as a daily mantra to raise resilient, confident children: "I can do all things."

Exodus 20:1–17   "The Ten Commandments"

In my opinion, the Bible is the library of life and the best guide for building character in ourselves and in our children. The Ten Commandments lay out clear expectations and guidance for living as moral and decent human beings.

Jeremiah 29:11   "Confidence in God's Plan"

When we rely on the Lord and declare him as our Creator, we can stand confidently on his promise of a good life. Encourage your children as you encourage yourself to trust God. He plans for us to have fun and be fulfilled. A well-balanced life depends not only on work and rules but also on prosperity and a good future. God desires that we place our hope in him.

2 Timothy 1:7   "Mental State"

Our mind is a powerful tool. Mothers are stronger than anyone can imagine. Mental strength leads to physical and spiritual strength. God fills our spirit with the power of love to lead us to be good, strong mothers. Keep fear and limiting beliefs from your heart, mind, and soul. It is okay to practice self-care and to take a break from routine to have some fun. Practicing these things keeps us in a healthy state of mind.

Psalm 103:5-6   "Be a Youthful Eagle Mom"

Being an Eagle Mom doesn't just mean setting rules, doing chores, or keeping the house clean. It also means maintaining a positive mindset and outlook on life. It means finding joy in being as merry as a child and maintaining a youthful spirit. Embrace your inner youth and share it with your children. It's ok to be silly!

Joshua 1:9   "Be Strong and Courageous"

This verse is a source of encouragement for the Eagle Mom. Raising a family can have its ups and downs, but by keeping this affirming scripture in our minds and hearts, we cultivate boldness, strength, and courage.

Proverbs 15:1   "Soft vs. Harsh"

This verse is essential for an Eagle Mom. It's vital to practice softness in motherhood. Avoid yelling or speaking harshly to your children. The worst thing in the world is to stir up feelings of bitterness or resentment in your child. Responding to our children and spouse in a soft manner does not show weakness. It shows good character and encourages respect and obedience.

Psalm 46:5   "Confidence in God; She Will Not Fail"

Even in tough times when we feel defeated, as Eagle Moms, we must trust in God through every adversity. When God is in the midst of your life, failures turn into success, trials become positive lessons, and weaknesses turn into strengths. The Eagle Mom mentality is to always overcome adversity.

PRAYER JOURNAL

This section can be pages where during quiet time a mom can jot down a:

prayer
reflection
thoughts
ideas

PRAYER

REFLECTION

THOUGHTS

IDEAS

PRAYER

_____

_____

_____

_____

_____

REFLECTION

_____

_____

_____

_____

_____

THOUGHTS

_____

_____

_____

_____

_____

IDEAS

_____

_____

_____

_____

_____

PRAYER

REFLECTION

THOUGHTS

IDEAS

PRAYER

_____
_____
_____
_____

REFLECTION

_____
_____
_____
_____

THOUGHTS

_____
_____
_____
_____

IDEAS

_____
_____
_____
_____

PRAYER

_____

_____

_____

_____

_____

_____

REFLECTION

_____

_____

_____

_____

_____

_____

THOUGHTS

_____

_____

_____

_____

_____

_____

IDEAS

_____

_____

_____

_____

_____

_____

PRAYER

_____
_____
_____
_____
_____

REFLECTION

_____
_____
_____
_____
_____

THOUGHTS

_____
_____
_____
_____
_____

IDEAS

_____
_____
_____
_____
_____

PRAYER

REFLECTION

THOUGHTS

IDEAS

PRAYER

_____

_____

_____

_____

_____

REFLECTION

_____

_____

_____

_____

_____

THOUGHTS

_____

_____

_____

_____

_____

IDEAS

_____

_____

_____

_____

_____

PRAYER

REFLECTION

THOUGHTS

IDEAS

PRAYER

REFLECTION

THOUGHTS

IDEAS

PRAYER

_____
_____
_____
_____
_____

REFLECTION

_____
_____
_____
_____
_____

THOUGHTS

_____
_____
_____
_____
_____

IDEAS

_____
_____
_____
_____
_____

PRAYER

_____
_____
_____
_____
_____

REFLECTION

_____
_____
_____
_____
_____

THOUGHTS

_____
_____
_____
_____
_____

IDEAS

_____
_____
_____
_____
_____

PRAYER

_____

_____

_____

_____

_____

REFLECTION

_____

_____

_____

_____

_____

THOUGHTS

_____

_____

_____

_____

_____

IDEAS

_____

_____

_____

_____

_____

PRAYER

_____
_____
_____
_____
_____

REFLECTION

_____
_____
_____
_____
_____

THOUGHTS

_____
_____
_____
_____
_____

IDEAS

_____
_____
_____
_____
_____

PRAYER

_____

_____

_____

_____

_____

REFLECTION

_____

_____

_____

_____

_____

THOUGHTS

_____

_____

_____

_____

_____

IDEAS

_____

_____

_____

_____

_____

PRAYER

_____

_____

_____

_____

REFLECTION

_____

_____

_____

_____

THOUGHTS

_____

_____

_____

_____

IDEAS

_____

_____

_____

_____

PRAYER

_____
_____
_____
_____
_____

REFLECTION

_____
_____
_____
_____
_____
_____

THOUGHTS

_____
_____
_____
_____
_____

IDEAS

_____
_____
_____
_____
_____
_____

PRAYER

_____
_____
_____
_____
_____

REFLECTION

_____
_____
_____
_____
_____

THOUGHTS

_____
_____
_____
_____
_____

IDEAS

_____
_____
_____
_____
_____

PRAYER

_____

_____

_____

_____

_____

REFLECTION

_____

_____

_____

_____

_____

THOUGHTS

_____

_____

_____

_____

_____

IDEAS

_____

_____

_____

_____

_____

_____

PRAYER

REFLECTION

THOUGHTS

IDEAS

PRAYER

_____
_____
_____
_____
_____

REFLECTION

_____
_____
_____
_____
_____

THOUGHTS

_____
_____
_____
_____
_____

IDEAS

_____
_____
_____
_____
_____

PRAYER

REFLECTION

THOUGHTS

IDEAS

PRAYER

_____
_____
_____
_____
_____

REFLECTION

_____
_____
_____
_____
_____
_____

THOUGHTS

_____
_____
_____
_____
_____
_____

IDEAS

_____
_____
_____
_____
_____
_____

PRAYER

_____

_____

_____

_____

_____

REFLECTION

_____

_____

_____

_____

_____

THOUGHTS

_____

_____

_____

_____

_____

IDEAS

_____

_____

_____

_____

_____

www.ingramcontent.com/pod-product-compliance
Lightning Source LLC
Chambersburg PA
CBHW080902120626
46555CB00008B/2912